Seriously Curious

EAGLE VALLEY LIBRARY DISTRICT
P.O. BOX 240   600 BROADWAY
EAGLE, CO 81631   (970) 328-8800

TOM STANDAGE is deputy editor of *The Economist* and the author of six books, including *A History of the World in 6 Glasses*. His writing has also appeared in the *New York Times*, the *Daily Telegraph*, the *Guardian* and *Wired*. *Seriously Curious* is the sequel to *Go Figure*, which he also edited.

SERIOUSLY CURIOUS

The Economist Explains

The Facts and Figures That Turn Our World Upside Down

Edited by

TOM STANDAGE

The
Economist   BOOKS

PUBLICAFFAIRS
New York

Copyright © 2018 by the Economist Newspaper Ltd
Cover design by Pete Garceau
Cover copyright © 2018 Hachette Book Group, Inc.

Hachette Book Group supports the right to free expression and the value of copyright. The purpose of copyright is to encourage writers and artists to produce the creative works that enrich our culture.

The scanning, uploading, and distribution of this book without permission is a theft of the author's intellectual property. If you would like permission to use material from the book (other than for review purposes), please contact permissions@hbgusa.com. Thank you for your support of the author's rights.

PublicAffairs
Hachette Book Group
1290 Avenue of the Americas, New York, NY 10104
www.publicaffairsbooks.com
@Public_Affairs

The Economist in Association with Profile Books Ltd. and PublicAffairs

Printed in the United States of America

Originally published in 2018 by Profile Books Ltd. in Great Britain.

First US Edition: November 2018

Published by PublicAffairs, an imprint of Perseus Books, LLC, a subsidiary of Hachette Book Group, Inc. The PublicAffairs name and logo is a trademark of the Hachette Book Group.

The greatest care has been taken in compiling this book. However, no responsibility can be accepted by the publishers or compilers for the accuracy of the information presented.

Where opinion is expressed it is that of the author and does not necessarily coincide with the editorial views of The Economist Newspaper.

While every effort has been made to contact copyright-holders of material produced or cited in this book, in the case of those it has not been possible to contact successfully, the author and publishers will be glad to make amendments in further editions.

The publisher is not responsible for websites (or their content) that are not owned by the publisher.

Print book interior Typeset in Milo by MacGuru Ltd

Library of Congress Control Number: 2018957599

ISBNs: 978-1-61039-993-7 (paperback), 978-1-5417-3012-0 (ebook)

LSC-C

10 9 8 7 6 5 4 3 2 1

Contents

Sexual selection: love, sex and marriage

Also on the menu: oddities of food and drink

Introduction: the case for being seriously curious

WHAT LINKS DETECTIVES, scientists, economists, journalists – and cats? The answer, of course, is curiosity. They all want to discover more about the world. But their curiosity is driven by more than just a desire to understand the way things are. They also want to understand the underlying mechanisms that explain how things got to be that way, so that they can anticipate, predict or explain future events. Detectives want to uncover people's motivations and solve crimes. Scientists want to devise new theories that will deepen their grasp of reality. Economists want to improve their understanding of the transactions that underpin human societies. Journalists want to create narratives that help people make sense of current affairs. Cats want to maximise their chances of getting their paws on more roast chicken.

All of them are constantly gathering evidence, devising theories and testing new avenues in pursuit of their goals. In all these fields, curiosity is not merely useful – it is vital. It is a willingness, or in fact a hunger, to discover new, previously unknown things. No wonder Thomas Hobbes called it "the lust of the mind". Curiosity provides the spur to gather more raw material for analysis, by probing the limits of what is known.

Alas, the information-driven, evidence-based way of looking at the world has lately fallen out of favour. In a "post-truth" world, knowledge is scorned, facts are optional (or can be challenged by "alternative facts") and reality can be distorted or ignored. But the seriously curious know that in the long run, reality will always prevail. Curiosity leads people towards a more accurate understanding of the world; only the terminally incurious can maintain a distorted or inaccurate worldview for long, and only then by walling themselves off from evidence that challenges their outlook. Curiosity is the royal road to truth.

So this book takes a stand, in its own small way, for the forces of curiosity, evidence and reason. It brings together unexpected explanations and fascinating facts from *The Economist*'s output of explainers and daily charts. Its mission is to show, through a series of entertaining examples, how logic and data can illuminate the hidden mechanisms that make the world work the way it does. Why do tennis players grunt? Why does polygamy make civil wars more likely? What is the link between avocados and crime? Why is there a shortage of sand? How does fracking boost birth rates?

Each of these questions is a miniature mystery story. Each one challenges you to imagine your own explanation, like a detective arriving at the scene of a crime. (You are probably wondering about those criminal avocados right now.) After a paragraph or two of context comes the explanation, and enlightenment dawns – or, just as satisfyingly, you discover that your theory was indeed the correct answer. Moreover, you now understand an aspect of how the world works better than you did before.

We hope this collection will stimulate and satisfy your curiosity. The very fact that you are reading this book at all, and have bothered to read to the end of this introduction, grants you admission, along with the detectives, scientists and cats, to the ranks of the seriously curious. Welcome to the club.

Tom Standage
Deputy Editor, *The Economist*
July 2018

Seriously curious: unexpected explanations to stretch your mind

Why polygamy makes civil wars more likely

Wherever polygamy is widely practised, turmoil tends to follow. The 20 most fragile states in the world are all somewhat or very polygamous. Polygamous nations are more likely to invade their neighbours. The polygamous regions of Haiti and Indonesia are the most turbulent; in South Sudan, racked by civil war, perhaps 40% of marriages involve multiple wives. One study, by the London School of Economics, found a strong link between plural marriage and civil war. How come?

Polygamy nearly always involves rich men taking multiple wives. And if the top 10% of men marry four women each, then the bottom 30% cannot marry at all. This often leaves them not only sexually frustrated but also socially marginalised. In many traditional societies, a man is not considered an adult until he has found a wife and sired children. To get a wife, he must typically pay a "bride price" to her father. When polygamy creates a shortage of brides, it massively inflates this bride price. In South Sudan, it can be anything from 30 to 300 cattle – far more wealth than an ill-educated young man can plausibly accumulate by legal means.

In desperation, many single men resort to extreme measures to secure a mate. In South Sudan, they pick up guns and steal cattle from the tribe next door. Many people are killed in such raids; many bloody feuds spring from them. Young bachelors who cannot afford to marry also make easy recruits for rebel armies. If they fight, they can loot, and with loot, they can wed. In a paper published in 2017, Valerie Hudson of Texas A&M University and Hilary Matfess of Yale found that a high bride price is a "critical" factor "predisposing young men to become involved in organised group violence for political purposes". Jihadist groups exploit this, too. One member of Pakistan's Lashkar-e-Taiba, which carried out the attack on Mumbai in 2008 that killed 166 people, said he joined the organisation because it promised to pay for his siblings to get married. Radical Islamist groups in Egypt have also organised (and helped to pay for) marriages for members. In northern Nigeria, where polygamy is rife, Boko Haram still arranges cheap marriages for its recruits.

Globally, polygamy is in retreat, but in some pockets support for it is rising. After America's Supreme Court legalised same-sex marriage in 2015, some people argued that plural unions should be next. According to Gallup, a pollster, the proportion of Americans who consider polygamy to be morally acceptable rose from 5% in 2006 to 17% last year, among the most dramatic jumps in the subjects it tracks. Campaigners in Kyrgyzstan, Turkmenistan and other central Asian states are seeking to re-establish men's right to take multiple wives. In Kazakhstan, a bill failed in 2008 after a female MP included an amendment stipulating that polyandry (women taking multiple husbands) also be allowed. Advocates claim that polygamy promotes social harmony by giving lusty husbands a legitimate alternative to infidelity. But the mayhem in places like South Sudan, Afghanistan and northern Nigeria suggests otherwise.

Why there is a shortage of sand

Sand is in high demand. In some parts of the world, people are going to increasing lengths to get their hands on the golden grains. A "sand mafia" in India intimidates locals in order to extract and transport the material. In Morocco and the Caribbean, thieves are stripping beaches bare. Even though fully accounting for illegally mined sand is not possible, sand is easily the most mined material in the world. According to the UN Environment Programme (UNEP), sand and gravel account for up to 85% of everything mined globally each year.

Modern cities are built with, and often on, sand. Most of it is used in the construction industry to make concrete and asphalt. No surprise, then, that Asia is the biggest consumer of sand. China alone accounts for half of the world's demand. That reflects the country's breakneck pace of construction: according to the United States Geological Survey, China used more concrete from 2011 to 2013 (6.6 gigatons) than America did in the entire 20th century (4.5 gigatons). Sand also has industrial uses: it is used to make glass, electronics, and to help extract oil in the fracking industry. Vast quantities of sand are dumped into the sea to reclaim land. Singapore, for example, has expanded its land area by more than 20% since the 1960s in this way. The Maldives and Kiribati have used sand to shore up their islands against rising sea levels. The UN forecasts that, by 2030, there will be over 40 "megacities" home to more than 10m inhabitants (up from 31 in 2016), which means more housing and infrastructure will need to be built. And sea levels will continue to rise. All of this means that sand will only become more sought after.

So why is there a shortage, when sand seems so abundant? The trouble is that desert sand is too smooth, and cannot be used for most commercial purposes. Australian sand was transported to a faraway desert to build Dubai's Burj Khalifa tower. Most countries also have rules in place about where, and how much, sand can be mined. But voracious demand has sparked a lucrative illegal trade in many rapidly developing countries. The result is that existing deposits are being mined more quickly than they can be naturally replenished, which is damaging the environment. Dredging causes pollution and harms local biodiversity, while thinning coastlines affect beaches' capacity to absorb stormy weather.

Fortunately, there are substitutes for sand: asphalt and concrete can be recycled, houses can be built with straw and wood, and mud can be used for reclamation. In rich countries, government policy will encourage a shift towards such substitutes. According to Britain's Mineral Products Association, for example, nearly a third of all housing material used in Britain in 2014 was recycled. Singapore is planning to rely on Dutch expertise for its next reclamation project, which involves a system of dykes and is less dependent on sand. In poorer countries, too, builders are likely to shift away from sand as its price rises. But unless law enforcement improves, that will be a very slow process, and the shortage of sand will persist.

How shoelaces untie themselves

Engineering brings great benefit to humanity, from bridges to computer chips. It has, though, had difficulty creating a shoelace that does not accidentally come loose. This was, in part, because no one truly understood why shoelaces come undone in the first place. But that crucial gap in human knowledge has now been plugged. Christopher Daily-Diamond, Christine Gregg and Oliver O'Reilly, a trio of engineers at the University of California, Berkeley, have worked out the mechanics of shoelace-bow disintegration. They have finally solved the mystery of how shoelaces untie themselves.

Technically, a shoelace bow is a type of slip knot that has, at its core, a reef knot. Like conventional reef knots, bows can be mistied as "granny" knots, which come undone more easily than a true reef does. But even a shoelace bow with a true reef at its core will fail eventually, and have to be retied. That is because walking involves two mechanical processes, both of which might be expected to exert forces on a shoelace bow. One is the forward and back movement of the leg. The other is the impact of the shoe itself hitting the ground. Preliminary experiments carried out by Mr Daily-Diamond, Ms Gregg and Dr O'Reilly showed that neither of these alone is enough to persuade a bow to unravel; both are needed. So they had to devise experiments which could measure and record what was going on while someone was actually walking. The "someone" in question was Ms Gregg, who endured numerous sessions on a treadmill so that the behaviour of her shoelaces could be monitored. Using cameras, and tiny accelerometers attached to the laces, the researchers realised that two things are important. One is how the act of walking deforms the reef at the centre of a bow. The other is how the different inertial forces on the straight-ended and looped extremities of the bow conspire to pull the lace though the reef in the way a wearer would when taking a shoe off.

During walking, the reef itself is loosened by the inertial forces of the lace ends pulling on it. This occurs as a walker's foot moves first forward and then backward as it hits the ground during a stride.

Immediately after that, the shock of impact distorts the reef still further. This combination of pull and distortion loosens the reef's grip on the lace, permitting it to slip. In principle, the lace could slip either way, giving an equal chance of the bow eventually undoing completely or turning into a non-slip knot of the sort that long fingernails are needed to deal with. In practice, the former is far more common. The reason turns out to be that the free ends of the bow can swing farther than the looped ends do. The extra inertial force this causes favours slippage in the direction of the longer of the free ends. To start with, the effect is small. But as the free end in question continues to elongate, the disparity in inertial force gets bigger – and, eventually, only two or three strides are needed to take a shoe from being apparently securely tied to being untied.

Probably, nothing can be done about this differential elongation. But it might be possible to use the insights Mr Daily-Diamond, Ms Gregg and Dr O'Reilly have provided to create laces that restrict the distortion of the reef at a bow's centre, and thus slow the whole process down. Understanding how laces untie themselves is, you might say, an important step on the way to inventing a solution.

Why the sea is salty

Seen from space, the Earth is a pale blue dot. Two-thirds of its surface is covered by water. But most of that water by far – around 97% – is salty. Of the 3% that is fresh water – which is the kind humanity needs to drink, wash, make things and (most of all) produce food – about two-thirds is locked up in glaciers, ice caps and permafrost. That leaves less than 1% of the planet's water easily accessible in rivers, lakes or aquifers. In short, the salinity of the oceans means useful water is scarce, while the less useful kind is abundant. So why is the sea salty?

The salt in the ocean mostly got there as the result of a process called weathering, which transfers mineral salts from rocks on land into the sea. Rain is not pure water, but contains small amounts of carbon dioxide absorbed from the air, which makes rainwater very slightly acidic. When this weak acid falls on land, tiny traces of minerals are dissolved from rocks into the water, and these minerals separate into charged particles called ions. These ions travel along with the water into streams, rivers and eventually into the ocean. Many of these mineral ions are subsequently removed from the sea water by marine plants and animals, but others remain in the water, and their concentration builds up over millions of years. Over 90% of the ions in sea water, accounting for about 3% of the ocean by weight, are sodium and chlorine ions, which are the chemical constituents of common salt. Other processes also play a role. Underwater volcanoes and hydrothermal vents discharge mineral salts into sea water. And isolated bodies of water with insufficient drainage may become increasingly salty through evaporation, which carries water away while leaving dissolved minerals behind. The Dead Sea (which contains about 30% mineral salts by weight) is the best-known example.

The natural processes that make the seas salty can be reversed by desalination technologies that turn sea water into fresh water. This involves either boiling and then recondensing water, or pumping it at high pressure through reverse-osmosis membranes that allow water molecules to pass, but are impermeable to larger mineral ions. Both processes are energy-intensive, however, though reverse osmosis has become far more energy-efficient in recent years. Accordingly, desalination plants are generally found in places where water is scarce but energy is cheap, such as the Middle East.

As climate change causes "global drying" – making some wet parts of the world wetter, and dry parts drier – demand for fresh water will intensify in the coming years; half the world's population is expected to live in water-stressed areas by 2050. Better water-management policies and more water-efficient agricultural practices (such as drip irrigation) are needed. Improvements to desalination technology would help too, by allowing mankind to tap the oceans' inconveniently salty water. "If we could ever competitively – at a cheap rate – get fresh water from salt water," observed President John F. Kennedy in 1961, "that would be in the long-range interests of humanity, which would really dwarf any other scientific accomplishment."

Why diamond production may be about to peak

In the frozen tundra of northern Canada, miners work day and night to extract diamonds from beneath the ground at Gahcho Kué. Owned by De Beers, it is the biggest new diamond mine to open in more than a decade. It may also be the company's last – De Beers has no plans to open another. Other companies have a few mines planned, but Bain, a consultancy, expects diamond production to peak in 2019, then begin a slow decline. Why is the world about to reach peak diamond production?

The modern diamond industry got going about 150 years ago, when a farmer's son found a diamond near the Orange River in South Africa. A diamond rush followed, causing a surge of production that threatened to send prices plummeting; the high price of diamonds depends on their scarcity. In 1888 Cecil Rhodes founded De Beers to consolidate the area's mines. The company would retain a stranglehold on supply for more than a century, limiting availability in order to maintain high prices. "Our only risk," Rhodes later declared, "is the sudden discovery of new mines, which human nature will work recklessly to the detriment of us all."

Much has changed since then. De Beers now controls only about one-third of the market. It regards any big discoveries, by itself or anyone else, to be unlikely. Explorers have sampled nearly 7,000 kimberlite pipes, the extinct volcanoes that brought most gem diamonds to the surface. Of these just 15% held diamonds and only 1% (about 60) contained enough to justify the cost of building a mine. Though exploration continues, most analysts reckon that the best deposits have now all been found.

For those who dig up diamonds, waning supply is a relief; it will help prop up prices. Brides continue to want diamond engagement rings: in America, De Beers reports, a quarter of young brides dreamed of their rings years before beginning a relationship. But there are signs that demand might falter. Those in the millennial generation earn less than their parents did at their age and are less interested in material luxury. They grew up as awareness of "blood diamonds", which are mined to fund conflict and are illegal, entered popular culture. Brides who want a diamond now have alternatives in the form of synthetic diamonds, which have improved in quality and become less costly to produce. De Beers and other miners are working to boost demand, with new advertising campaigns and slogans. But it helps that supply is not forever.

Why Boko Haram prefers female suicide-bombers

Boko Haram has used more female suicide-bombers than any other terrorist group in history. Of the 434 bombers the group deployed between April 2011 and June 2017, 244 of them, or more than half, have been definitely identified as female. More may have been. The Tamil Tigers, the previous holders of the gruesome record, used 44 female bombers over a decade, according to a study by Jason Warner and Hilary Matfess for the Combating Terrorism Center at West Point, an American military college. Boko Haram, whose insurgency has killed more than 30,000 people in north-east Nigeria and neighbouring countries since 2011 and displaced 2.1m, is therefore the first group to use a majority of female bombers.

Nigeria's government likes to say that Boko Haram has been "technically defeated". The group split into two factions in 2016, after Islamic State (IS) declared a preference for a more moderate leader, Abu Musab al-Barnawi, over Abubakar Shekau. The latter's tactics include using suicide-bombers to blow up mosques and markets, inevitably killing fellow Muslims. (Some analysts dispute the idea of factions, arguing that Boko Haram has always been made up of different cells.) But the group is far from vanquished, even though it has been forced out of towns since Muhammadu Buhari, a former military dictator, reclaimed the presidency in 2015. In July 2017 the branch affiliated to IS killed 69 members of an oil-exploration team. Indeed, the group's suicide-bombings were especially lethal in 2017, after a relative lull in 2016. During June and July alone they killed at least 170 people, according to Reuters, a news agency. The jihadists are sending more children to their deaths too: the UN counted 83 used as human bombs in 2017, four times the total for 2016. Two-thirds of them were girls.

The suicide-bombers sent by Boko Haram are, however, less lethal than those used by other groups, say Mr Warner and Ms Matfess. This is partly because around a fifth of them detonate their explosives when confronted by soldiers, killing only themselves.

Yet still the group sends attackers to Maiduguri, the city where the insurgency began, to target the university, markets and camps for the displaced. It is no coincidence that its use of female bombers rose sharply after the kidnapping of the 276 "Chibok Girls" from their school in April 2014. Boko Haram realised the propaganda value of women: the use of supposed innocents as lethal weapons has a powerful shock factor. They arouse less suspicion (at least they did when the tactic was first deployed, if no longer) and can more easily hide explosives underneath a voluminous hijab. And by sending women to blow themselves up, Boko Haram also saves its male fighters for more conventional guerrilla-style attacks.

Some of the women may be willing, if brainwashed, jihadists. Many, though, are believed to be coerced into strapping on bombs. One did so with a baby on her back. Some may see it as a way out of an abusive life as one of Boko Haram's "wives", plenty of whom are raped by their "husbands". Those who give themselves up to the authorities rather than detonating their bombs often face a lifetime of stigma, as their families and communities may be unwilling to take them back. So whether the women kill anyone or not, Boko Haram sows fear and division – exactly as it intends.

Move over, oil. Which countries have the most lithium?

Lithium is a coveted commodity. Lithium-ion batteries store energy that powers mobile phones, electric cars and electricity grids (when attached to wind turbines and photovoltaic cells). Demand is expected nearly to triple by 2025. Annual contract prices for lithium carbonate and lithium hydroxide for 2017 have doubled, according to *Industrial Minerals*, a journal. That is attracting investors to the "lithium triangle" that spreads into Argentina, Bolivia and Chile. This region holds 54% of the world's "lithium resources", an initial indication of potential supply before assessing proven reserves.

Despite having similar-sized lithium resources, there are vast differences in output between the three countries. Chile produced 76,000 tonnes in 2016, more than twice as much as Argentina. Bolivia only managed to sell a measly 25 tonnes. Such differences are emblematic of how the South American trio treat enterprise and investment more generally. Market-friendly Chile is far ahead in rankings for ease of doing business, levels of corruption, and the

Below the salt
Lithium resources, tonnes, m
January 2017

Australia 2.0   Canada 2.0

| Argentina 9.0 | Bolivia 9.0 | Chile 7.5 | China 7.0 | US 6.9 | Other 3.6 |

Lithium-producing countries
Selected

	Lithium production 2016, tonnes LCE*	Foreign direct investment Net inflows, 2015, as % of GDP	Ease of doing business index 2016 ◄1=best 190►	Corruption Perceptions Index, 2016 ◄1=best 176►
Argentina	30,050	2.0	116	95
Bolivia	25 (sales only)	1.5	149	113
Chile	76,000	8.5	57	24
Australia	74,250	2.9	15	13

Sources: US Geological Survey; Roskill Information Services;
Comibol; World Bank; Transparency International

*Lithium carbonate equivalent

quality of its bureaucracy and courts. Even so, production growth has flattened, allowing Australia to threaten its position as the world's top producer.

It has been decades since anyone thought of Argentina as business-friendly. Cristina Fernández de Kirchner, a populist president who governed until December 2015, made things harder. But under her successor, Mauricio Macri, Argentina has been hastening to make up lost ground. Bolivia has barely begun to exploit its resources. Its investment regime suffers from "lack of legal security, weak rule of law, corruption and murky international arbitration measures", according to America's State Department. In the battle for lithium-triangle supremacy, it has a long way to go.

Why the global arms trade is booming

In February 2017 the emirate of Abu Dhabi held the International Defence Exhibition and Conference (IDEX), the Middle East's largest arms fair. The four-day event was a roaring success, playing host to 1,235 exhibitors and a record number of delegates. On the last day, the United Arab Emirates announced $5.2bn worth of weapons purchases from suppliers including France, Russia and America. The Gulf state's hunger for big guns is hardly exceptional. A study by the Stockholm International Peace Research Institute (SIPRI), a think-tank, found that transfers of big weapons from 2012 to the end of 2016 reached their highest volume for any five-year period since the end of the cold war. Why is the global arms trade doing so well?

The frail security balance of an increasingly multipolar world has many countries worried. Since the end of the cold war, scholars have found that greater instability – both internal and external – has tended to be correlated with a rise in military spending, as intuition would suggest. What has changed in recent years is that a larger share of the money is going towards imports: in contrast with the 2000s, when the West's armies undertook the bulk of the fighting in Afghanistan and Iraq, many nations sucked into this decade's disputes lack military muscle and have no domestic industry capable of building it up. With America less eager to be the world's policeman, they see a greater need for buying their own kit. Vietnam, which borders the South China Sea, imported three times more weaponry in the period from 2012 to the end of 2016 than in the previous five years. Saudi Arabia's purchases grew by 212% and Qatar's by 245%.

But the trade is also underpinned by a push on the supply side. America, which sells arms to more than 100 countries, dominates the market. As technology improves, it is helping to retool developing nations' arsenals with modern gadgets, such as GPS guidance and automated systems. Its exports grew by 42% from 2008 to 2015. Other exporters see a lucrative market too. China, known in the

1990s for its knock-offs of Western equipment, has emerged as a top-tier supplier. South Korea sells aircraft and warships to Latin America. Russia is building on its cold-war legacy business.

The proliferation of conventional weapons is a source of volatility in itself. Yet measures to contain them have been feeble. Unlike nuclear treaties, conventional-arms-control regimes focus on making sure weapons are not sold to irresponsible users, rather than promoting disarmament. Even within this narrower scope, the efficacy of such measures remains unproven. The UN-led Arms Trade Treaty, the first global attempt at regulating the business, came into force in December 2014. China and Russia are not signatories; America has yet to ratify it. Together, these three countries account for more than 60% of exports. Existing regional control instruments, such as the EU Code of Conduct on Arms Exports, have a patchy record of blocking controversial sales. In some regions, including Asia and the Middle East, there are no such treaties. Meanwhile, America's plans to increase military spending may prompt others to go shopping again. Expect arms trade shows – along with the arms trade – to continue to boom.

What do think-tanks do?

"According to such-and-such, a think-tank," is a phrase familiar to readers of any newspaper, not least *The Economist*. Sharp quotes, intriguing facts and bold new policy proposals are attributed to the mysterious tanks (as is plenty of rubbish). What exactly are these outfits, which churn out reports on everything from Brexit to badgers?

The "think-tank" label became popular in the 1950s, by which time there were already plenty of such organisations in existence. Many of America's most venerable examples, including the Brookings Institution and the Carnegie Endowment for International Peace, were founded in the early 20th century. Britain's Royal United Services Institute, a military-analysis outfit, was created in 1831 by the Duke of Wellington. But think-tanks really blossomed in the second half of the 20th century. Researchers at the University of Pennsylvania reckon there are now nearly 7,000 of them worldwide.

In essence, think-tanks aim to fill the gap between academia and policymaking. Academics grind out authoritative studies, but at a snail's pace. Journalists' first drafts of history are speedy but thin. A good think-tank helps the policymaking process by publishing reports that are as rigorous as academic research and as accessible as journalism. (Bad ones have a knack of doing just the opposite.) They flourished in the 20th century for two reasons. Governments were expanding everywhere, meaning there was lots of demand for policy expertise. And the arrival of 24-hour news created an insatiable appetite for informed interviewees. The same trends are now causing think-tanks to take off in developing countries.

Yet the world may have reached peak think-tank. The University of Pennsylvania's researchers found that in 2014 the number of new think-tanks declined for the first time in 30 years. One reason is that donors nowadays prefer to make project-specific grants, rather than funnelling money into mere thinking. Another is increased competition. Professional consultancies such as McKinsey publish a fair bit of brainwork, and members of opinionated "advocacy organisations" can make for more compelling interviewees than balanced think-tankers. So some think-tanks are rethinking themselves. The Pew Research Centre describes itself as a "fact-tank", focusing on information rather than policy recommendations. And the Sutton Trust calls itself a "do-tank" – not just coming up with ideas, but putting its own recommendations into practice.

How to measure the black market for cigarettes

In May 2017 Britain joined a growing number of countries in which cigarettes can only be sold in plain packs. Tobacco companies claim that the move will boost the sales of contraband cigarettes by making them trickier to spot. Working out whether that is true or not means tracking how black-market sales change. But how can such sales be measured?

There are about a dozen ways to do it, of which three are the most commonly used, says Hana Ross of the University of Cape Town. The first is a comparison of the number of cigarettes sold legally (from records on cigarette taxes paid) with the number of cigarettes consumed (which is calculated from surveys asking people how much they smoke). The gap between the two figures gives an estimate for the size of the black market. The second commonly used method is to ask smokers where they have bought cigarettes and how much they have paid; smokers may also be asked to show the most recent pack they have bought. A price lower than that of legally sold brands suggests a contraband sale; and some smokers openly admit that they have bought contraband cigarettes, or show a tell-tale pack.

The third method is to look at discarded cigarette packs and calculate what proportion of them look like black-market purchases (they may be missing their tax stickers, for example, or display a brand that is not officially registered). Discarded packs can be collected from vendors who sell cigarettes by the stick, from litter in the streets, or by rummaging through rubbish in bins or picking them up from refuse-collection trucks. ("We dress them as if they are going into space", says Ms Ross about the recruits who rummage through the rubbish heaps, wearing protective clothing.)

Each of these methods has its weakness. Smokers may, for example, be reluctant to mention purchases of cigarettes they know to be contraband. They may also claim to smoke less than they actually do (especially if researchers come round soon after a major anti-smoking campaign). Ideally, multiple methods should be applied in parallel to get a better estimate of total black-market sales, and how they change over time. Such studies are being conducted in a growing number of countries. Just because a sale occurs in the shadows does not mean it is impossible to cast a smouldering light on it.

Mapping the rise and fall of witch-hunting

"A witch! A witch! We have found a witch, may we burn her?" asks a marauding mob during a scene in *Monty Python and the Holy Grail*, a 1975 comedy film. "How do you know she is a witch?", the king's guard inquires. "She looks like one," comes the reply. The accused witch's defence is met with little sympathy. "They dressed me up like this. This isn't my nose. It is a false one," she cries in vain. That parody is remarkably close to the truth. Between the 14th and 18th centuries about 80,000 people were tried for witchcraft in Europe. They were not all old, scraggly-looking women: 15% of Scottish witches were men, and their average age was 42.

Their myriad alleged crimes were often trivial. A neighbourhood disagreement might escalate into accusations of sorcery if someone suffered a misfortune, such as a premature death in the family, after a quarrel. Around half of the accused were executed, usually by hanging or by being burnt at the stake. European witch trials fell out of fashion around 1770. In recent decades, interest in them has focused mainly on re-enactments for hobbyists and tourists. But the subject has also bewitched a small group of scholars, who have combed through the surprisingly detailed data sets available on the practice and have formulated theories to explain why, when and where such trials occurred.

In 2004 Emily Oster, an economist now at Brown University, published a paper arguing that witch trials were linked to economic shocks. Accusations of witchcraft were most prevalent during the "Little Ice Age", a period of particularly bitter winters in Europe beginning in 1590, which caused crops to fail and incomes to fall. Ms Oster speculated that medieval village-dwellers responsible for feeding poor older women in their communities may have denounced them as witches in an effort to save scarce resources. During a 164-year-long spell beginning in 1563, some 3,500 alleged witches were tried in Scotland, the second-highest rate per person in Europe. Based on Ms Oster's theory, that period should have been characterised by poor weather and poor harvests. But a working paper by Cornelius Christian, an economics professor at Brock University in Canada, found that the Scottish climate was actually unusually balmy during that period, leading to bumper crop yields. That led him to the opposite conclusion from Ms Oster's: people accused of witchcraft could only be persecuted with the co-operation of elites, he reasoned, who only had enough free time to get involved in witch trials when resources were plentiful.

Other researchers take a different view. A paper by Peter Leeson and Jacob Russ of George Mason University argues that religious tensions, not the weather, put witch-hunters on the prowl. They gathered statistics from 43,000 European witch trials, primarily drawn from the mountainous areas near Lyon in France, Lucerne in Switzerland and Freiburg in modern-day Germany. Of these, three-fifths occurred during the period from 1560 to 1630, known as the "Great Hunt", which was characterised by horrifying atrocities: in Würzburg, Bavaria, for instance, 400 people were executed on a single day. The authors attribute this hysteria to the aftermath of the Protestant Reformation. Witch trials were most common, they found, in areas where Catholic and Protestant churches enjoyed comparable levels of support and were locked in a struggle for converts. Conversely, such trials were much rarer where one creed or the other predominated. Mr Leeson and Mr Russ noted a striking similarity to modern American presidential elections, in which the two major parties focus on closely contested "swing states" while ignoring those where one has an insurmountable advantage.

Perhaps witch trials served a similar function during the Great Hunt to the role of political campaigns today: instead of competing to show voters they offer protection from terrorists and criminals, 16th-century religions competed to show potential converts they offered protection from witches. On this view, the witch-hunting equivalent of Florida (America's biggest swing state) appears to have been Strasbourg, in France: 30% of all witch trials on the continent occurred within 300 miles (500 km) of the city. There is a deeper parallel. Witch trials led to the murder of tens of thousands of innocent victims. Modern politicians frequently court voters

Double, double toil and trouble
European witchcraft, 1300–1850

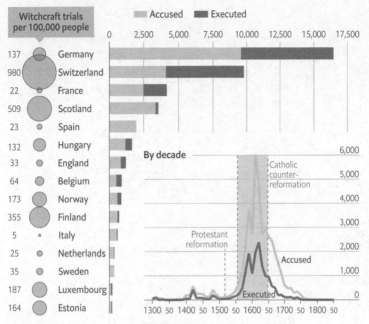

Source: "Witch Trials", by Peter Leeson and Jacob Russ, *Economic Journal*, August 2017

by warning of the perils posed by hidden enemies lurking in their midst. Voters might be well advised to consider whether the targets of the resulting policies are any guiltier than those accused of consorting with Satan just a few hundred years ago.

Globally curious: peculiar proclivities from around the world

Why spaghetti is smuggled across the Sahara

The shifting sands of the Sahara have long been crossed by trade and smuggling routes. Traffickers send people and drugs north over the desert. But they have a problem: what should they put in their empty trucks as they head back south? A popular answer, it would seem, is pasta. Some sources reckon that, apart from people, pasta is the most smuggled product (by weight) to cross the desert. Drug trafficking and gunrunning may earn fatter margins. But many smugglers diversify their loads by pushing penne. Why?

In part, the trade is fuelled by subsidies in north African countries. Algeria, for example, spends about $28bn a year keeping down the prices of food and energy. In Libya, which also subsidises food prices (though somewhat erratically, because of the civil war), 500g of pasta can be bought for as little as $0.15. In Timbuktu, an ancient city in Mali, hundreds of miles to the south-west, the same bag of pasta might fetch 250 CFA francs (the currency used in several west African states), which is equivalent to $0.50. In Senegal or some of the posher parts of Bamako, Mali's capital, it is worth even more: about 800 CFA francs, or $1.50.

Another incentive to smuggle is found in west Africa. Under the region's customs union, imports of pasta face a tariff of 20% and value-added tax of 15%. So smugglers of contraband pasta can easily undercut legal suppliers. Smugglers rarely answer surveys, so the facts are hard to pin down. But a study carried out in 2015 by the Economic Research Forum, a think-tank based in Egypt, found that pasta was the main product going across the Sahara from Algeria to Mali, accounting for about one-third of the trade. The researchers reckoned that smugglers earned profits of 20–30%.

The illicit pasta trade is not just making its mark in countries south of the Sahara, but also on the desert itself. As they ply their trade, many smugglers have taken to poking sticks of spaghetti into the sand as waymarks.

Why so many places are called Guinea – and turkeys don't come from Turkey

Guinea. Equatorial Guinea. Guinea-Bissau. Papua New Guinea. The Gulf of Guinea. Guinea, Virginia. Guinea, Nova Scotia. The world has more Guineas than a pirate's treasure chest. What explains the prevalence of the name?

Etymologists cannot agree on the origin of the word "Guinea". Some trace it to a word in Tuareg, a Berber language, for black people: *aginaw*. Others think it originally referred to Djenné, a trading city in modern-day Mali. In the 15th century, Portuguese sailors used "Guiné" to describe an area near what is today Senegal, and by the 18th century, Europeans used "Guinea" to refer to much of the west African coastline. As colonisers carved up the continent, many European nations controlled their own places called Guinea. At independence, French Guinea became Guinea, Spanish Guinea became Equatorial Guinea, and Portuguese Guinea became Guinea-Bissau. West Africa was a major source of gold, hence the name "guinea" for the British gold coin. In 1545, on the other side of the world, Yñigo Ortiz de Retez landed on an island north of Australia. Struck by the resemblance between its inhabitants and people from west Africa, the Spanish explorer named the island "New Guinea". The word "papua" probably comes from the Malay *papuwah*, meaning "frizzled", perhaps a reference to the islanders' hair.

In addition to the various places, there are also animals: the guinea pig, most famously, and the guinea fowl. The guinea pig comes not from any of the Guineas in Africa, but from South America. Muddled Europeans may have confused Guinea with Guyana, today South America's only English-speaking country. Guyana has nothing to do with Guinea: its name probably comes from a native word meaning "land of many waters". Some scholars, however, propose an alternative etymology for the guinea pig: the rodents were brought to Britain on "Guinea-men", trading ships that shuttled between Britain, South America and Guinea.

The guinea fowl, for its part, did come from west Africa. But it, too, has a complicated history. The birds were originally introduced to Britain via the Ottoman empire and so were called "turkeys". Later, early English colonists in America confused the native birds there with the African fowl, and called them "turkeys" too. (In fact, they are a larger and entirely separate species.) All in all, it is a linguistic mess. It is unclear where the word originally came from, but it was a series of historical accidents and misunderstandings during the colonial period that led to the modern world's proliferation of guineas.

Why New Zealand has so many gang members

For a quiet country, New Zealand has a peculiar problem with gangs. It is reckoned to have one of the highest membership rates in the world. In a population of 4.7m, police count over 5,300 mobsters or "prospects" who are angling to join. Cumulatively, that makes the groups larger than the army. Bikers like the Hells Angels and offshoots from Australian gangs are among its 25 recognised groups, but two Maori crews dominate: Black Power and the Mongrel Mob. Members signal their allegiance by sewing patches onto leather jackets or branding themselves with dense tattoos. A closed fist marks Black Power, which took its name from the American civil-rights movement, and a British bulldog signifies the Mongrels. In all, indigenous Maori people make up three-quarters of the country's gangsters.

They have dominated the gang world since the 1970s, when many moved to the cities, where they endured discrimination and ended up in poverty because of difficulties finding work. Opportunities have improved since, but life is often harder for indigenous people than for other New Zealanders. They do worse in school, suffer poorer health and die younger. Some turn to the gangs in search of power or oblivion. Some become members in jail, forced to join a crew simply to protect themselves. Others seek something more positive: *whanau*, or community. Many recruits join simply because their fathers are members. The gangs, they say, are like a family. New Zealand's high rate of gang membership is, in short, a reflection of the difficulties faced by Maori people.

Most New Zealanders never encounter this underworld, because violence generally occurs between the gangs, and their turf wars have abated in recent decades. Today much of the gangs' criminal activities relate to drugs. Corrections officers say that foreign syndicates use the biker groups to distribute methamphetamines. Gang members account for more than 14% of the charges of conspiracy to deal methamphetamines, and of murder, laid in New Zealand. They fill about a third of prison cells. This does much to explain why more than half of all the nation's inmates are Maori, although they make up only 15% of the population.

The popularity of methamphetamines within the gangs has also undermined them. A handful of leaders have banned the drug's consumption after witnessing the damage it has wrought on their communities. Some have attempted to clean up their branches in other ways. The groups used to have horrific reputations for gang rape, but Black Power now prohibits it, and has also moved to reduce domestic violence more generally. Female associates of Black Power and the Mongrel Mob report that their lives are much improved. But while reform-minded members of the more established groups are maturing, a younger set of Los Angeles-style street gangs is now on the rise in New Zealand, many of them Maori and Polynesian. Their bling-obsessed teenage recruits are violent and unpredictable. New Zealand's high rate of gang membership seems likely to endure.

Why the exorcism business is booming in France

Philippe Moscato, an exorcist, walks from room to room in a large Paris flat, sprinkling blessed water and offering incantations. "Spirits away!", he calls out, telling otherworldly pests that their attacks will, from now on, be futile. He informs the homeowner that the air will improve after his work is done, with the entire apartment block likely to benefit. For the ritual, which lasts an hour, Mr Moscato pockets €155 ($190). He says he despooks properties in Paris a few times each week; roughly once a week, he conducts an exorcism of a person. He is not alone. Look online and a host of private exorcists, healers, mediums, kabbalists, shamans and energiticians offer similar services, for fees as high as €500 per ceremony. Some offer to help a business out of a bad patch, or to restore love to a failing relationship. Many help with supposed hauntings of properties. One self-declared exorcist near Paris says he earns as much a €12,000 a month (before tax) by working 15-hour days, including consultations by phone. Why is the exorcism business booming in France?

According to the exorcists, they thrive because customers get much-needed benefits from the rituals. Mr Moscato, for example, describes an "avalanche" of demand after the terrorist attacks in France late in 2015. He suggests that three parts of France are particularly vulnerable to "black magic" – Paris, Lyon and the French Riviera, where local mafia are said to be active – and that this can be countered by sufficiently strong exorcists. Alessandra Nucci, a writer on Catholic matters who has attended a course run by the International Association of Exorcists (IAE) in Rome, says there are more and more private operators in Europe who charge for their services. She suggests they are filling a vacuum left by priests reluctant to do the job: the church "has, for too long, neglected exorcisms, despite strong demand from the public", she says.

The demand is real, but reasons for it are mixed. Roughly half of the customers for one exorcist near Paris, for example, are immigrants, notably Africans ready to turn to fee-charging and charismatic exorcists rather than church-sanctioned ones. Other clients, such as the owner of the Paris flat visited by Mr Moscato, sign up after hearing of friends who did so, in part – though not only – for the entertainment of witnessing the ritual. They are not church-goers and would have been unlikely to ask a priest to bless their home. Many are encouraged by the ease of finding and booking an exorcist online. It could be that demand for private practitioners previously existed but is now more public thanks to the internet, where exorcists can easily advertise their services. Television shows, such as Fox's *The Exorcist*, could also be encouraging customers to try a ritual.

Exorcism remains a niche business, but could become more popular among those not of the traditional church, such as immigrants. House blessings, like those conducted by Mr Moscato, appear to be harmless entertainment. But risks exist: occasionally victims of violent rituals, including children, have been killed in beatings that are supposed to chase evil spirits from a person. The more responsible fee-charging exorcists say a diagnosis or exorcism of a person should happen only after a patient has consulted a doctor or psychiatrist. In general, those who pay for such rituals appear to believe they get some kind of result, just as others opt for homeopathic medicines or astrological readings and expect some positive effect. Any supposed benefit follows from the fact that the customer first believes in the service – which is true of many other businesses, too.

Why China has the world's worst flight delays

China's airports are a marvel. During the past decade, nearly ten new ones have opened every year. Sleek, spacious, modern buildings, outfitted with the latest technology, they can shimmer like visions from the future. Yet they are also objects of dread and loathing for just about anyone who has spent time passing through them. It is not the buildings themselves so much as what they represent: long waits. China's airports may be some of the world's most elegant, but they are also global leaders in flight delays. Of the world's 100 busiest airports, the seven that suffer the longest delays are all in China, including the country's major hubs in Beijing, Shanghai and Shenzhen. At the 13 Chinese airports that rank among the world's top 100, flights are delayed by 43 minutes on average. The global norm, excluding China, is 27 minutes. The only other airports that come close to rivalling China for tardiness are the three that serve the crowded skies around New York: JFK, LaGuardia and Newark.

Congestion is only a partial explanation for China's delays. China is already the world's second-biggest aviation market, with about half a billion passengers per year, and the industry is still expanding at a double-digit rate. It is destined to overtake America as the world's busiest market (based on passenger numbers) within a decade, according to the International Air Transport Association. But when looking at numbers of flights, China actually has a surprising amount of slack. Just one of its airports is among the world's 20 busiest for flights (Beijing Capital International, which ranks seventh). Chinese airports, in other words, tend to have fewer flights, and bigger planes carrying more passengers. That should, in principle, make it easier to avoid delays. What's more, given that Chinese airports generally have ample runway space and state-of-the-art air-traffic-control systems, they should be better at getting planes into the air on time.

Why is China's record so poor? The first reason is that its airports err on the side of extreme safety. At many big airports around the world, intervals between flights (whether taking off or landing) have been compressed to as little as 30 seconds. In China they are often

Cleared for take-off
Airports with the highest average number of departures per month

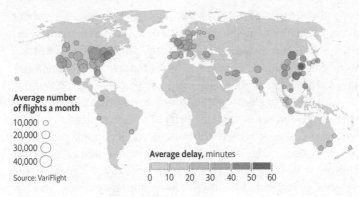

**Average number
of flights a month**

10,000 ○
20,000 ○
30,000 ○
40,000 ○

Source: VariFlight

Average delay, minutes

0   10   20   30   40   50   60

as long as two minutes, even when there is a backlog of planes. In the summer months, when weather is wetter, the timeliness of Chinese flights deteriorates markedly (see chart). Just two out of every five flights departed as scheduled in July 2017. Nevertheless, at a time of such rapid growth in air travel, the caution of China's air-traffic controllers is understandable. There have been no significant accidents on their watch over the past five years.

A second factor ought to be more readily solvable. The military controls roughly three-quarters of airspace in China, and shunts civilian traffic aside. When the air force takes flight, commercial planes have no choice but to wait on the runway, sometimes for hours. The government has long vowed to do a better job of integrating civil and military management of airspace, and to release more air corridors for commercial use. Yet improvements have, so far at least, been imperceptible. It is a touchy subject. Airlines rarely inform passengers that military exercises are the reason for late departures, instead citing generic air-traffic controls or inclement weather, even on clear days. But official figures published in 2017 revealed that military activity was responsible for about a quarter of delays. It all adds up to more time stuck inside China's gleaming (but frustrating) airports.

Why Somaliland is east Africa's strongest democracy

Drop a pin on a map of eastern Africa, and the chances are it will not land on a healthy democracy. Somalia and South Sudan are failed states. Sudan is a dictatorship, as are the police states of Eritrea, Rwanda and Ethiopia. President Yoweri Museveni of Uganda has ruled uninterrupted since 1986, and has passed a law to remove a constitutional age limit so he can cling on longer. Elections in Tanzania have never ousted the Party of the Revolution; it and its predecessor have governed continuously since independence in 1961. Even Kenya, once the region's most vibrant and competitive democracy, is struggling. In October 2017 Uhuru Kenyatta was re-elected president with 98% of a preposterously flawed vote. In this context, tiny Somaliland stands out. In November 2017 citizens of this internationally unrecognised state elected a president in its sixth peaceful, competitive and relatively clean vote since 2001. This unparalleled record makes it the strongest democracy in the region. How has this happened?

A peculiar history helps. Somaliland was a British protectorate, before merging with Italian Somalia in 1960 to form a unified Somalia. It broke away in 1991, and now has a strong sense of national identity. It was one of the few entities carved up by European colonists that actually made some sense. Somaliland is more socially homogeneous than Somalia or indeed most other African states, and greater homogeneity tends to mean higher levels of trust between citizens. A decade of war against the regime of Siad Barre in Mogadishu, Somalia's capital, reduced Somaliland's two largest cities to rubble, yet produced a flinty patriotic spirit. And the Somali National Movement (SNM), which led the fighting, cultivated an internal culture of democracy. Its leadership changed five times in nine years, and transferred power to a civilian administration within two years of victory.

But it is the absence of international recognition that may matter most. Muhammad Haji Ibrahim Egal, the president of Somaliland from 1993 to 2002, argued in 1999 that recognition would be dependent on the country's pursuit of democracy. He proceeded to devise a constitution that was put to a popular referendum in 2001. For fear of encouraging other separatist movements in the region, the international community, following the African Union, has never obliged by recognising Somaliland. But rather than stunting democracy, this response ensured that democratisation spread from the bottom up. Donors often demand democratic reforms from African countries as a condition of financial aid. Because unrecognised Somaliland is cut off from most external assistance, the social contract between government and citizens has become unusually strong. Democracy evolved out of a series of mass public consultations – clan conferences – which endowed it with an unusual degree of legitimacy. The system's most striking feature is the upper house of clan elders, known as the "Guurti", which ensures broadly representative government and underpins much of the country's consensual political culture.

Somaliland's democracy is by no means spotless. Corruption is endemic, and the media are seldom critical. The influence of the clans has been muted but not eradicated. And elections are repeatedly delayed. The vote in November 2017 was overdue by more than two years, by which time all branches of government had outlived their mandates. The lower house had been sitting for 12 years; the Guurti has sat unelected since it was formed in 1993. And there may be even bigger challenges in the future. In 2017 Somaliland signed agreements with the United Arab Emirates to build a new port and a military base at the coastal town of Berbera. The former, valued at over $400m, was the country's largest-ever investment deal. Nation-building on a shoestring helped keep Somaliland's politicians relatively accountable, and helped to maintain the delicate balance between clans. That may not be the case for much longer. But in the meantime, it is a beacon of democracy and an example to its neighbours.

Why yurts are going out of style in Mongolia

If the best-known emblem of Mongolia is its mighty 13th-century conqueror, Genghis Khan, the second best-known is probably the humble nomadic dwelling known in English by the Turkic word *yurt*. Legend has it that Genghis Khan himself ruled his vast empire from – suitably enough – an especially large one, nine metres in diameter. The Mongolian word for yurt, *ger*, has come to mean "home" and it also forms the root of the verb "to marry". Why, then, does this central and beloved bit of cultural patrimony seem to be going out of style?

With their collapsible lattice frames made of wood and their highly efficient felt insulation, yurts are both warm and transportable. Indeed, many nomads have transported their yurts to the edges of the capital, Ulaanbaatar. On three sides of the city, ramshackle neighbourhoods are populated by migrants from all across Mongolia's vast countryside. These steadily growing hillside areas are universally referred to as "*ger* districts", and those white domes are their most prominent feature when viewed from the heart of the city. But fewer than half of the residents in these districts actually live in yurts. Most have taken the 700 square metres of land allotted to them by national law and built simple fixed structures of wood, brick or concrete instead.

The number of rural dwellers migrating to cities increased suddenly with Mongolia's transition, in 1990, from a Soviet-imposed communist system to democracy. Since 2000 the influx of herders to Ulaanbaatar, by far the country's largest city, has grown especially fast. Drought, together with an increased frequency of the phenomenon known in Mongolian as a *dzud (*an especially dry summer followed by an especially harsh winter that livestock cannot survive), have made herding more difficult. At the same time, Ulaanbaatar's rapid development has made it more attractive as a source of both job opportunities and services, including health care and education. But city officials have so far failed to provide basic infrastructure to the growing *ger* districts. The pit latrines that serve well enough for yurt dwellers in sparsely populated rural areas are ill-suited to the densely packed settlements on Ulaanbaatar's edges. Neither are the *ger* districts connected to city heating systems, forcing residents to burn coal for their cooking and heating needs. This generates horrendous pollution, and a good deal of grumbling among residents of the city's built-up areas.

Added to this is the fact that once they give up herding for city life, migrants have less use for one of the yurt's main advantages: portability. All this explains the results of a survey of Ulaanbaatar's *ger*-district residents, published in 2015: 72% of respondents said they would move into an apartment if they could. And even in the countryside Mongolians are heeding the siren song of modern living and being lured out of their yurts, albeit at a slower rate. Between 2010 and 2015, the proportion of households living in yurts declined by 1.3 percentage points, according to Mongolia's national statistics bureau. It will take some time, but the noble yurt looks like it is on its way to joining Genghis Khan as a symbol of Mongolia's proud past.

Which cities have the highest murder rates?

Cocaine is grown primarily in South America, and trafficked to the world's biggest market, the United States, via Central America and the Caribbean. The land routes originate mainly in Colombia, and pass through the small nations of El Salvador, Honduras and Guatemala before traversing Mexico. It is little wonder, then, that Latin America remains the world's most violent region not at war. According to data from the Igarapé Institute, a Brazilian think-tank, 43 of the 50 most murderous cities in the world in 2016, and eight of the top ten countries, are in Latin America and the Caribbean. (War zones, where numbers are hard to verify, are excluded.) Conflicts between gangs, corruption and weak public institutions all contribute to the high levels of violence across the region.

The top of the ranking has not changed. In both 2015 and 2016, El Salvador was the world's most violent country, and its capital, San Salvador, was the most murderous city. However, the 2016 numbers do represent a slight improvement: the national murder rate fell from 103 killings per 100,000 people in 2015 to 91 the following year, and San Salvador's murder rate from 190 to 137. Most analysts credit a clampdown by government security forces for this reduction, though tough-on-crime policies do little to address the underlying causes of gang violence. A similar downward trend was evident in neighbouring Honduras: San Pedro Sula, which for years wore the unwelcome crown as the world's most murderous city, ranked third.

However, spikes in violence in neighbouring countries suggest that anti-gang policies are merely redistributing murders geographically rather than preventing them. Acapulco, a beach resort on Mexico's Pacific coast, recorded 108 homicides per 100,000 people in 2016, placing it second behind San Salvador. That reflects the nationwide trend: Mexico's overall rate rose from 14.1 killings per 100,000 people to 17. That figure nearly equals the previous violent peak of Mexico's drug wars, in 2011. As a result, six Mexican cities rank among the top 50, three more than did so a year earlier.

Mean streets
Homicides per 100,000 population, 50 highest cities*, 2016 or latest | National rate

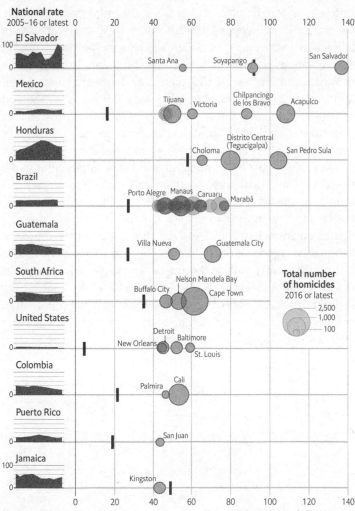

National rate
2005–16 or latest

El Salvador
Santa Ana, Soyapango, San Salvador

Mexico
Tijuana, Victoria, Chilpancingo de los Bravo, Acapulco

Honduras
Choloma, Distrito Central (Tegucigalpa), San Pedro Sula

Brazil
Porto Alegre, Manaus, Caruaru, Marabá

Guatemala
Villa Nueva, Guatemala City

South Africa
Buffalo City, Nelson Mandela Bay, Cape Town

Total number of homicides
2016 or latest
2,500
1,000
100

United States
New Orleans, Detroit, Baltimore, St. Louis

Colombia
Palmira, Cali

Puerto Rico
San Juan

Jamaica
Kingston

Source: Igarapé Institute

*With populations of 250,000 or more

The middle of the list is dominated by Brazil: the world's second-biggest cocaine consumer is home to half of all cities in the ranking. That mostly reflects its large population. During 2016, violence shifted from place to place within Brazil: the murder rate fell in the largest cities, but increased in smaller ones. In Maraba and Viamão, homicides rose by 20% in a year, whereas in São Paulo, Brazil's most populous city, murders fell by 55% from 2014 to 2015. Unlike in Mexico and Central America, there is evidence of a slight overall improvement: the national homicide rate fell from 29 per 100,000 in 2014 to 27 in 2015, the latest year for which data are available. Nonetheless, by sheer virtue of its size, Brazil reigns as the world's overall murder capital: 56,212 people were killed there in 2015.

Only two countries outside Latin America contain cities in the top 50: the United States and South Africa. In America, the only rich country on the list, a spike in homicides propelled two more cities, Detroit and New Orleans, to join St Louis and Baltimore, which also figured on 2015's list. Each has a rate that is around ten times the national average of 4.9 homicides per 100,000 people. South Africa is the only country outside the Americas in this ranking. Two new cities, Nelson Mandela Bay and Buffalo City, have been added to the list, mainly because data collection is improving in the country. The homicide rate in South Africa climbed by 5% last year, though other violent crime dropped.

Why young Britons are committing fewer crimes

Crime in Britain has been falling, as in many rich countries. In England and Wales the decline has been dramatic: since the mid-1990s the number of offences has fallen by half. Vehicle theft has dropped by 86% since 1995 and burglaries by 71%. The most reliable measure of lawbreaking, the Crime Survey for England and Wales, is based on the experiences of victims, rather than perpetrators. But evidence from elsewhere suggests that within the broader decline in lawbreaking is another even more striking decline: that in crime committed by young people.

The number of youngsters aged between ten (the age of criminal responsibility in England and Wales) and 17 entering the criminal-justice system for the first time has tumbled, down by 84% since 2006. By contrast, the number of adults has declined by just 46%. Those figures partly reflect the fact that the police have abandoned performance targets that had encouraged them to pick up misbehaving youngsters; catching spray-painting teenagers is easier than nabbing burglars. But the decrease has been so dramatic that it almost certainly points to children being more law-abiding today than they used to be. Other measures support this thesis. According to the victims of violence interviewed for the crime survey, between 2006 and 2016 the proportion who thought their attacker was aged 16 or under fell by almost half, from 14% to 8%. And between 2012 and 2015 the proportion of pupils at secondary schools were who temporarily suspended fell from 8.3% to 7.5%. Declines in the numbers of youngsters arrested have also been seen in countries such as Germany, the Netherlands and America.

Youngsters have become more law-abiding for similar reasons as their elders. Items that they used to steal, such as televisions and car radios, have fallen in value, so taking them is no longer worthwhile. Security measures such as burglar alarms have made it harder to break into houses. Central locking and other security features have made stealing cars trickier. Better and smarter policing has helped too. But some factors may have helped to drive down crime among young people specifically. In particular, they are living more abstemiously. The proportion of British children who said that they had ever experimented with drugs fell by half between 2001 and 2014. Among adults, the figure barely shifted. In 2014 just 38% of 11–15 year-olds admitting to having tried alcohol; in 1988 over 60% said that they had tried drinking.

This more sober lifestyle affects crime rates in three ways, argues Tim Bateman of the University of Bedfordshire. Less drug-taking means less law-breaking to fund purchases. Crimes related to the possession and acquisition of drugs also decline. And children are less likely to commit crimes when they are not drunk or high. Technology may also be helping to make the world less crime-ridden. Spending hours on computers and smartphones provides a benign alternative to getting up to no good. According to a study in 2012 by researchers from the London School of Economics, British children spend more time online and start going online at an earlier age than the European average. These trends bode well for the future: research shows that law-abiding children are more likely to turn into law-abiding adults.

How car colours reflect Britain's national mood

Car buyers are said to choose vehicles that reflect their personality. In Britain the colour may also reflect the national mood. In the late 1990s Britons bought cars in bright primary colours, perhaps mirroring the optimism of the early years of Tony Blair's New Labour administration. In the following years, as the economy ticked along steadily, they went for sensible greys and silvers. As economic hardship followed the financial crisis, sentiment turned darker as black cars predominated.

The popularity of white cars is harder to explain. Once so unpopular that police forces stopped using them because resale values were so low, white cars go hand in hand with Britain entering new territory when David Cameron's coalition government starting making inroads with policies that reversed the country's gloomy mood. Or perhaps draining a car of colour is another way of not making a firm choice. At least the reversion to black is easier to

Back to black

Britain, new car registrations, by favourite colour

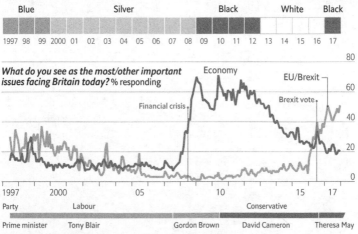

Sources: Society of Motor Manufacturers and Traders; Ipsos MORI

comprehend, as the haplessness of Theresa May's government and worries over Brexit have darkened the outlook for Britain's drivers.

Why Swedes overpay their taxes

How abnormal are Swedes, and other people in the Nordic region, in paying tax? A general stereotype for Europe holds some truth: unlike tax-shy southern Europeans, those in the far north pay up readily to get comprehensive, efficient government services – and to live in societies with unusually equitable income distribution. In Sweden, even after years of slashing high taxes (an inheritance tax went in 2005, another for wealth disappeared in 2007 and corporate tax is low, at 22%), the share of the national income claimed by the state remains high. The OECD, a club of mostly rich countries, reckons Sweden's government spent over 51% of GDP in 2014. Income-tax rates for the well-off can be as high as 57%. And the Swedes comply. Sociologists, economists and others have long debated this readiness to cough up for the common good. Lutheran beliefs about the importance of supporting the whole community might be a factor, along with a strong sense of cultural homogeneity. Or maybe the generations spent huddling together to survive long, dark winters played a role.

February 2017 brought a new puzzle, however, with evidence that some Swedes had been deliberately overpaying their taxes. Official figures published that month showed tax revenues had poured in far faster than expected during 2016. Sweden's government ended up with a budget surplus of 85bn kronor ($9.5bn) for the year, and nearly half of that, 40bn kronor, was the result of tax overpayments by firms and individuals. This appeared to be deliberate. It also posed a conundrum for civil servants responsible for making repayments and managing the funds. What was going on?

This was not evidence, in fact, of a new or extreme culture of Nordic eagerness for paying tax. Instead the explanation is financial, a bizarre result of the existence of negative interest rates. Starting in March 2015, Sweden's central bank kept rates below 0%, as did other Swedish banks, in a broad effort to avoid deflation. At the same time, the government promised to pay a positive interest rate – 0.56% – for any funds that had been overpaid in tax, upon their return to the taxpayer. Even though this interest payment was subsequently cut to zero, individuals and companies were better off storing their savings with the government in the form of overpaid tax, rather than watching them shrink in the bank as a result of negative interest rates.

Officials and politicians would usually crow about a growing budget surplus. But Sweden's official bean-counters are not cheering. Borrowing from taxpayers (by taking in their over-payments, and then paying them back) costs more than raising funds in other ways. Nor is it entirely clear how quickly those who have overpaid will demand their money back, which makes it tricky to manage the flow of money. Sweden's negative interest rates, which had been expected to rise in early 2018, were instead extended, which suggests that overpayment of taxes will also go on longer than expected. It sounds like the sort of problem a government in southern Europe would be delighted to have. In Sweden, however, officials would much prefer taxpayers to cool it – and pay a bit less in tax.

Mapping the world's mega-rich

High-net-worth individuals
Global wealth*, $trn

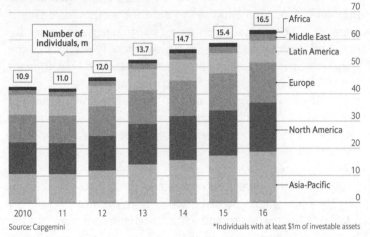

Source: Capgemini   *Individuals with at least $1m of investable assets

The global number of high-net-worth individuals (HNWIs) grew by 7.5% to 16.5m in 2017, according to the World Wealth Report by Capgemini, a consulting firm. HNWIs have at least $1m in investable assets, excluding their main home, its contents and collectable items. Total HNWI wealth came to $63.5trn in 2017, with the highest proportion concentrated in the Asia-Pacific region. The expansion of wealth in the Asian-Pacific region slowed to 8.2% year-on-year, as a result of declines in the performance of stockmarkets in China and Japan. But if Asian wealth (the biggest source of new future growth) grows by 9.4% a year, global HNWI wealth will exceed $100trn by 2025.

Why nobody knows how many Nigerians there are

Nigeria is Africa's most populous country, a designation it wears with pride. It had more than 182m citizens in 2015, according to the World Bank, and is poised to have the world's third-largest population, behind India and China, by 2050. But those figures are based on Nigeria's 2006 census, which probably exaggerated the number of people. Parliamentary seats and central government money are handed out to states based on population, giving politicians an incentive to inflate the figures. In 2013 the head of the National Population Commission (NPC), Festus Odimegwu, said that neither the 2006 census nor any previous one had been accurate. He resigned soon afterwards (the government at the time said he was fired).

Counting Nigerians has been controversial since the colonial era. The country was stitched together from two British colonies: a largely Christian south and a Muslim-dominated north. In the lead-up to independence in 1960, the British were accused by southerners of manufacturing a majority in the north, which they were thought to favour. In 1962 unofficial census figures showed population increases in some south-eastern areas of as much as 200% in a decade. The full data were never published and northern leaders held a recount, which duly showed they had retained their majority (their region had apparently grown by 84%, rather than the originally estimated 30%). This politicking led to coups, the attempted secession of what was then known as the Eastern Region, and a civil war.

The north–south divide has remained salient; there is still an unwritten rule that the presidency should alternate between a northerner and a southerner. Allegations that the north has manipulated its way to a majority continue. The censuses of 1973 and 1991 were annulled. In 2006 arguments flared when 9.4m people were counted in the northern state of Kano, compared with just 9m in Lagos, the commercial capital. The Lagos state government conducted its own, technically illegal, census and came up with a figure of 17.5m (probably a vast overestimate). A new national census has been repeatedly delayed. The NPC's estimate that it will "gulp" 223bn naira ($708m) may mean the count is put off indefinitely.

Even using other methods, Nigeria's population has proved tricky to pin down. Africapolis, a French-funded research project, employed satellite mapping to estimate the population of towns and cities in 2010. It found that several cities, mostly in the north, had hundreds of thousands fewer people than the 2006 census counted. But even those data are not entirely trustworthy: it later transpired that the researchers had underestimated urbanisation in the densely populated Niger delta. Until there is an accurate, impartial census it will be impossible to know just how many Nigerians there really are. That means government policy will not be fully anchored in reality – and it will not be possible to send resources where they are most needed.

Why Chinese children born in years of the dragon are more successful

Dragons have long been revered in Chinese culture. As a result, children born in the dragon years (or "dragon children") of the zodiac calendar are thought to be destined for success in later life. Naci Mocan and Han Yu, two economists at Louisiana State University, decided to probe this superstition.

The researchers note that Chinese parents certainly seem to prefer raising dragon children than, say, sheep children. The number of babies born in China spiked in 2000 and 2012, the two most recent years of the dragon. Birth rates in Taiwan, Hong Kong, Singapore and Malaysia follow a similar pattern. But China's "one-child policy" made it difficult for parents to time the births of their children to correspond with years of the dragon, which reduced the effect of the zodiac calendar on births.

Children fortunate enough to be born in dragon years seem to flourish at school. The authors looked at the test scores of some

Dragonborn

China

Live births, m

1991 Stricter enforcement of "one-child policy" introduced

Years of the dragon

Dragon childrens' performance relative to peers, points in middle-school exams*

Estimate

95% confidence interval

Before controlling for parental expectations

Maths
Chinese
English

After controlling for parental expectations

Maths
Chinese
English

Sources: "Can Superstition Create a Self-Fulfilling Prophecy? School Outcomes of Dragon Children of China" by Naci Mocan and Han Yu, Louisiana State University; government statistics

*On exams with average scores of 70

15,000 Chinese secondary-school pupils, and found that relative to their peers, dragon children received better grades in both their Chinese and their English exams. Moreover, analysis of a different data set showed that they were 11 percentage points more likely to go to university than others. These findings held true when accounting for family background, cognitive ability and self-esteem. What is different about dragon children, the researchers argue, is how much their parents believe in them.

Parents of dragon children tend to spend both more money and more time educating them. Such parents are more likely to speak to teachers and enrol their children in kindergarten. They also dish out more pocket money. At the same time, dragon children are given fewer chores around the house. When these factors are controlled for, the academic edge of dragon children disappears; there is, it seems, nothing inherently special about being born in a dragon year. Instead, the success of dragon children, the authors argue, is a self-fulfilling prophecy.

Sexual selection: love, sex and marriage

Why the sperm-bank business is booming

Once a practice associated with students looking to make a quick buck, sperm donation has penetrated the ranks of big business. The AIDS epidemic that began in the 1980s ended the informality surrounding the business, and as the costs and risks around testing and handling donated sperm increased, medics pulled out and entrepreneurs swiftly filled the gap. Today savvy sperm banks – particularly those that are able to export – can make a very decent income supplying a growing and changing market. How do businesses make money in the jizz biz?

Two things have provided entrepreneurs with fertile ground. First, a patchwork of regulatory intervention means that in certain countries the flow hasn't kept up with demand. In several places, including Britain, anonymous donation has been outlawed. In other countries donors cannot be paid. Both reasons help explain why sperm banks in such places often struggle to recruit donors; the long waiting lists caused by low donor-counts can lead to customers shopping abroad. Second, as acceptance of modern family structures grows, so too does demand for a key missing ingredient. Where the vast majority of customers were previously heterosexual couples who were having trouble conceiving, today many if not most are either lesbian couples or single women. In some countries such women are forbidden from being treated with donated sperm, encouraging them to shop abroad. The smartest businesses have picked up on such gaps in the market and sell their stuff direct to sperm banks and clinics that struggle to recruit donors in their home markets. Possibly an even bigger money-spinner is selling directly to end-users. Thanks to the internet, dry-ice and DHL, customers can now shop for sperm from more or less anywhere and have it delivered to their homes.

Some American sperm banks boast that a donor can make up to $1,500 per month, which presumably requires near-abstention from personal pleasure. The normal rate for a single donation is around $100. One donation can usually be split into as many as five vials, which in turn sell for between $500 and $1,000 each. Most customers buy several. Despite the costs involved – notably for recruiting donors, testing and retesting, storage and marketing – the margins are engorged. Still, sperm banks have to work hard to compete for customers; some distinguish themselves by emphasising the safety and security of their "product". Others focus on the "user experience" by modelling their websites on popular dating sites, where customers can filter candidate donors by particular features such as eye colour, education or hobbies. Some banks will charge extra for information ($25 for a childhood picture and so on) or sell premium subscriptions – giving extra information and early access to new donors – for hundreds of dollars more.

Even the most radical free-market liberals struggle with the question of whether sex cells (and other bodily tissue) should be as easy to trade as any other product. To protect the interests of donor-conceived children, there is a strong case for having basic regulation in place to ensure that all vials are tested for certain diseases before they can be sold. But morally driven policies about who can conceive using donated sperm are both discriminatory and, in the age of e-shopping, ineffective. More generally, overly restrictive policies, shortages and higher prices (they have roughly doubled over the past decade) seem to be driving customers to other sources of supply, including an international grey market that is distinctly dodgy. National regulators would do better to jump on the bandwagon rather than trying to stand in its way.

How porn consumption changed during Hawaii's false alarm

The threat of nuclear holocaust, familiar to Americans who grew up during the cold war, is alien to most today. On Saturday January 13th 2018 fears of annihilation re-emerged. At 8.07am Hawaiians awoke to a startling emergency alert on their phones, which warned them that a ballistic missile was inbound and that they should seek immediate shelter. It was not until 8.45am that the government revealed that the alert was sent in error, and that there was no threat. The episode, though horrifying for those involved, provides a unique window into the human psyche. Unsurprisingly, Google searches for phrases like "bomb shelter" surged during those confusing minutes. But less predictably, another website also saw its traffic fluctuate wildly that morning: Pornhub.

Data from the world's most-viewed pornography site show that visits from Hawaii plummeted immediately after the missile alert hit, and did not regain their usual levels until around 15 minutes after the threat was revealed to be a false alarm. But as Hawaiians

What a relief

Hawaii, Jan 13th 2018, traffic to Pornhub compared with an average Saturday, % difference

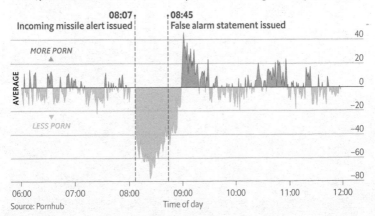

Source: Pornhub

returned to their regular lives, many apparently took to the internet to alleviate their pent-up anxieties. Traffic, as compared with an average Saturday, peaked at 9.01am, when visits to the lewd website rose to 48% above their normal levels. Hawaiians' exuberance did not last long. By 9.30am, Pornhub data show it was business as usual in America's 50th state.

Why transgender people are being sterilised in some European countries

The road to sex reassignment covers some very difficult terrain, ranging from hormone treatment and possibly surgery, to social stigma and discrimination. In many European countries, gaining legal recognition for reassignment is extremely difficult. Citizens of Malta, Ireland, Denmark and Norway can simply notify the authorities of their decision. Elsewhere the process requires judicial consent or even the diagnosis of a mental disorder. Switzerland, Greece and 18 other countries (mostly in eastern Europe), also have a final hurdle: sterilisation. Why is this the case?

The requirement for sterilisation has dark echoes of eugenics. In the early 1970s Sweden became the first country in the world to allow transgender people to reassign their sex legally. But it enforced a strict sterilisation policy, on the grounds that such people were deemed to be mentally ill and unfit to care for children. (The World Health Organisation still lists "transsexualism", which it describes as "a desire to live and be accepted as a member of the opposite sex", as a mental and behavioural disorder.) Sweden's eugenics laws, which imposed sterilisation on women deemed mentally defective or otherwise handicapped to a degree "which makes them incapable of looking after their children", lapsed only in 1976, after 42 years. But sterilisation remained a condition for sex reassignment until 2013. By this time, other countries had followed suit and adopted the same approach.

Amnesty International estimates that the European Union is home to around 1.5m transgender people (those whose gender identity differs from their biological sex). Though Europe is widely seen as progressive on LGBT rights, transgender rights specifically still lag. The processes involved in sex reassignment vary greatly between countries, most of which require a complex combination of medical interventions and legal paperwork. Compulsory sterilisation is perhaps the most controversial measure, provoking criticism from LGBT activists and the United Nations. States in which the idea of a man giving birth, or a woman fathering a child, are considered inconsistent with family values may cling to these clauses. But in April 2017, the European Court of Human Rights ruled in favour of three French complainants on the grounds that forced sterilisation violated their right to a private and family life – something guaranteed by the European Convention on Human Rights.

The court's ruling binds France, and it suggests that the law in the 20 countries that still insist on sterilisation violates the convention on human rights. But it does not compel these countries to reform. Activists say it is likely to require several similar court cases before the continent reaches any kind of legal consensus. Understanding of transgender people is spreading, though, including the knowledge that many of them do not seek surgery. And in some countries, gender is becoming a less important characteristic for organising society: the Dutch parliament is considering whether official documents should record gender at all.

How opinions on acceptable male behaviour vary by age, sex and nationality

Harvey Weinstein was the tip of a very large iceberg. In the month after multiple allegations of sexual assault against the prominent film producer became public, a series of powerful men were accused of sexual assault and harassment of co-workers. In just a few weeks, the #MeToo hashtag on social media, used to mark posts about similar experiences suffered by ordinary people, was used some 5m times. This avalanche of accusations increased awareness of the prevalence of sexual harassment: 49% of male respondents to a poll by NBC News and the *Wall Street Journal* in October 2017 said that the news had made them think about their own actions around women. Yet there is no clear consensus on exactly which behaviours cross the line. Instead, people in different countries and age groups appear to use very different definitions.

During October and November 2017 YouGov, a pollster, surveyed people in five Western countries about whether a series of behaviours by men towards women constitute sexual harassment. The questions ranged from actions that are often innocuous, such as asking to go for a drink, to overt demands for sex. The range of views was vast. One consistent pattern that emerged was a generation gap. In general, younger respondents were more likely to think that a behaviour crossed the line than their older peers were. For example, over half of British women under 30 said that wolf-whistling was unacceptable. Less than a fifth of those over 64 felt that way.

Between men and women, differences of opinion emerged for specific questions. Both sexes tended to have similar views on whether a man who places his hand on a woman's lower back or comments on her attractiveness has gone too far. However, female respondents were much less tolerant of men looking at women's breasts than their male counterparts were: among Americans 64 and older, for example, half of women but just a quarter of men said they would consider such ogling sexual harassment. A third source of variation was nationality. Swedish men, for example, seem to

My eyes are up here

"Would you consider it sexual harassment if a man, who was not a romantic partner, did the following to a woman?"

Surveyed Oct–Nov 2017, % stating "always" or "usually", by age and sex

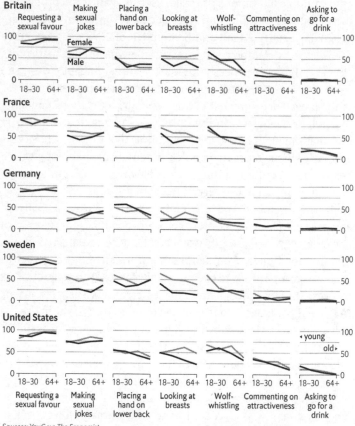

Sources: YouGov; *The Economist*

feel entitled to make sexual jokes around women: only a quarter of them said such behaviour would be harassment. In contrast, three-quarters of American men thought it was unacceptable. Similarly, a quarter of French women under 30 believe that even asking to go for a drink is harassment, whereas almost none of their counterparts in Britain and Germany share that view.

The magnitude of the reaction to the accusations against Mr Weinstein made clear that a reckoning with abuses by men in the workplace was long overdue. But given how little agreement exists about the definition of sexual harassment, employers seeking to ensure a comfortable work environment may need to be more explicit about the boundaries of acceptable behaviour than they may have previously realised was necessary.

What porn and listings sites reveal about Britain's gay population

Half a century after Britain's Parliament passed the Sexual Offences Act of 1967, which partially decriminalised homosexual acts, gay life is flourishing more than ever. The country boasts the world's gayest legislature, according to Andrew Reynolds, a professor of political science at the University of North Carolina at Chapel Hill: some 45 of the 650 members of Parliament elected in June 2017 were openly gay or bisexual. Britain is also tied with Sweden as the least homophobic country on the Gay Travel Index, an annual ranking produced by Spartacus World, a gay holiday guide.

Even though Britons see gay and lesbian politicians and fictional characters more and more often on television, there is still a surprising lack of data about where gay life is most concentrated. Polls typically find that about a quarter of people say they feel some attraction to the same sex, but just 2% of respondents to the Annual Population Survey identify themselves as something other than straight – a group too small to give an accurate regional picture. But analysis of two datasets can provide a clearer view.

The first attempts to measure where gay people live, and was provided by the insights team at Pornhub.com, a widely viewed pornography website. The video-streaming service attracts 5m visitors from Britain each day, 5.6% of whom watch gay content (excluding lesbian porn, whose main audience is straight men). When broken down by county, the data show very little geographic variance: 97% of the population lives in a region that is within one percentage point of the national average. Since some groups of people watch more porn than others, the numbers cannot reveal how many gay Britons there are. However, this does imply that gay people are very evenly distributed around the country.

The second dataset aimed to depict gay visibility. This involved scraping records of venues and events from a handful of listings websites, selecting only those that catered specifically to gay or bisexual people. These records are likely to be incomplete, since

Send your location
Britain, 2017

Same-sex organisations and events

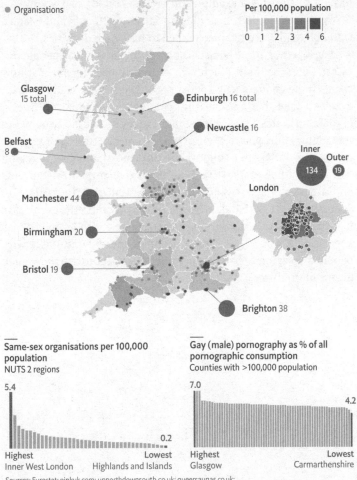

• Organisations

Per 100,000 population
0 1 2 3 4 6

Glasgow
15 total

Edinburgh 16 total

Newcastle 16

Belfast
8

Inner
134

Outer
19

Manchester 44

London

Birmingham 20

Bristol 19

Brighton 38

Same-sex organisations per 100,000
population
NUTS 2 regions

5.4

0.2

Highest   Lowest
Inner West London   Highlands and Islands

Gay (male) pornography as % of all
pornographic consumption
Counties with >100,000 population

7.0

4.2

Highest   Lowest
Glasgow   Carmarthenshire

Sources: Eurostat; pinkuk.com; upnorthdownsouth.co.uk; queersaunas.co.uk;
pridesports.org.uk; wikishire.co.uk; lgbtconsortium.org.uk; Pornhub.com; *The Economist*

these lists are mostly user-generated, and gay bars are shutting down at a startling rate. *The Economist*'s data team found 675 organisations in total, ranging from club nights to cycling teams to church groups. There were many varieties, but their locations were heavily clustered. For example, inner west London had 25 times as many events per person as did Scotland's highlands and islands. Other busy, liberal cities also tended to have high densities.

Put together, these datasets suggest that lots of gay people live in rural areas without much sign of their presence. But that now seems to be changing. Specialist dating apps have made it much easier to meet partners nearby. Thanks to a gradual decline in bigoted attitudes, older gay people are more willing to move to the countryside, where there is also a fair smattering of gay-run hotels and B&Bs. After London, the next most publicly gay region was found to be rustic Devon, home to five annual Pride events and a queer arts festival at Dartington Hall that took place in September 2017. Ceri Goddard, who helped organise the event, says it "reminded locals that amongst them there are thousands of gay and lesbian people". As Britain becomes more comfortable with people displaying their sexuality openly, expect to see more such events in rural areas.

Attitudes to same-sex relationships around the world

In the West, few civil-rights movements have prevailed so quickly and comprehensively as the campaign for gay rights. In America, support for same-sex marriage shot up from 27% in 1996 to 64% in 2017 – faster than the rise in acceptance of interracial marriage beginning in the late 1960s. Ireland has gone from having few openly gay public figures to legalising gay marriage and having a gay prime minister. But what about the rest of the world? How do Chinese or Peruvian people feel about gay rights? For that matter, what about the inhabitants of Angola? Figures compiled by the International Lesbian, Gay, Bisexual, Trans and Intersex Association (ILGA) provide some tantalising clues.

Take one straightforward measure – the proportion of people who strongly agree with the proposition that equal rights and protections should be applied to everyone, including people attracted to others of their sex. Not surprisingly, a majority of Americans, Spaniards and Swedes put themselves in that camp. A bit more surprisingly, Americans are somewhat less keen on gay and lesbian rights than are Argentinians, Brazilians, Chileans or Mexicans.

Most astonishing are the results from Africa. Although north African countries like Algeria, Egypt and Morocco are broadly opposed to gay rights, sub-Saharan Africa looks rather liberal. Attitudes in Angola, Ghana, Kenya and Mozambique are comparable to those in America – and much more liberal than attitudes in China or Japan. South Africa, as befits the fifth country in the world to legalise gay marriage, appears to be hotter on gay rights than America or Britain.

Can this possibly be true? ILGA's figures come from RIWI, a firm that uses an unusual method of soliciting opinion called "random domain intercept". When somebody types in an incorrect internet domain name, they might land on a site owned by RIWI, which (after checking the user is not a bot) asks them to complete a

Straight solidarity

"Equal rights and protections should be applied to everyone, including people who are romantically or sexually attracted to people of the same sex", % strongly agreeing
July to September 2017

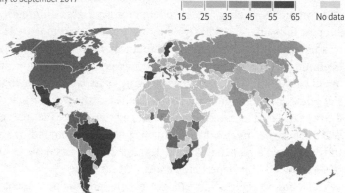

Source: ILGA-RIWI Global Attitudes Survey on Sexual, Gender and Sex Minorities, 2017

survey. So this is a poll of fat-fingered internet users, not of people in general. And attitudes to homosexuality in, say, rural Angola are highly likely to differ from attitudes among the connected classes in Luanda. Still, the results are suggestive. If a goodly number of internet-using, middle-class Africans are coming round to gay rights, that is something. The battle for gay rights in Africa and Asia is going to be a long, hard slog. A beachhead, however small, will help a lot.

Why couples do more housework than single people

Single people beware: if and when you move in with someone, you will probably end up doing more housework. Across the rich world, men and women in couples spend more time doing housework than single people. The extra burden is greatest for women in partnerships, who do on average five more hours of housework per week than single women. Men in couples do just half an hour more. For most, household chores are boring and tedious. So why do those in couples spend more time on them – and why is the difference bigger for women?

The answer is not simply that couples are more likely to have children, who create mess. Cristina Borra of the University of Seville, Martin Browning of the University of Oxford and Almudena Sevilla of Queen Mary University of London looked at detailed data on how people spend their time in America, Britain and Australia. When they excluded time spent caring for children and looked at couples without children, the differences remained. Perhaps, they suggest, the difference is down to the type of person who becomes part of a couple. The tidy(ing) sort might be more likely to partner up than the messy. And perhaps women in couples spend less time bread-winning, leaving more time for bread-baking.

The researchers looked at people over time, as they moved into couples, and at the differences between routine housework chores, like cooking, cleaning and tidying; and non-routine housework, like making repairs around the house. Looking at routine housework, they found that almost half the difference for women is driven by the fact that the sort to join a couple does more housework in the first place. But it is different for men. The kind of man who spurns routine housework is more likely to couple up. The extra housework such men do comes in the form of DIY or managing the family finances. The economists debunk the idea that women spend fewer hours on paid work – even when they account for differences, the chore inequality persists. It's not that women have more time; they just do more housework.

If people in couples choose to do more housework than singletons, that is their business. Perhaps it is harder to be messy when there is someone watching over your shoulder. Well-cooked meals may be more enjoyable consumed as a pair. The gender inequality this research suggests is more concerning, however, not only in itself, but also because it could be holding back women in the workplace. Routine tasks are harder to fit around a hectic work schedule, whereas building a shelf can be done at the weekend. Men might dismiss the difference as a matter of taste, assuming, perhaps, that women prefer doing the housework, or value its fruits more highly. Women might even be responding to their partners' possible deficiencies, at cooking, say. But women, rather than enjoying housework, may instead be conforming to society's expectations. An earlier study, published in 2012, found that whereas the amount of housework men did seemed to vary depending on how much they hated it, women experienced no such luxury.

What men and women think about their partners' careers and housework

Across the Western world, women greatly outnumber men in lower-level jobs, such as clerical and administrative positions, whereas managerial and senior jobs are mostly held by men. This gender gap at work is largely due to the "motherhood penalty" that women's careers suffer after they have children. But another more subtle factor could be part of the problem.

The Economist and YouGov, a pollster, asked people in eight countries how they balance career and family. Men were on average only half as likely as women to think that, in their family, the majority of household and child-care duties fell on the woman's shoulders. And they were more likely than women to say that such tasks were split equally. Respondents were also asked which partner had scaled back at work when their first child arrived, by reducing working hours or by switching to a part-time or a less demanding job (for example, a role that required less travel or overtime). Another perception gap emerged. In each country, both

---

The perception gap
Average of surveyed countries, Feb 2017, %

Between you and your partner, who is mostly responsible for household tasks and child care?
Adults with spouses or partners

Did either you or your partner scale back your career after you had your first child?
Adults with children under 18 living at home

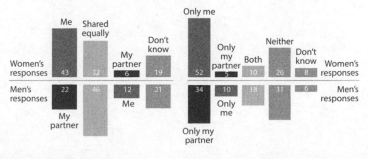

Sources: YouGov; The Economist

men and women were less likely to say that their partner had made adjustments than members of the opposite sex were to say they had made adjustments themselves.

Perceptions in France differed most: 55% of women said that they, and only they, had slowed down at work, twice as high as the share of men who said that only their partners had done so. The difference was smallest in Denmark, the country that had the largest shares of both men and of women saying that neither partner had made adjustments. (Denmark has one of the world's most generous child-care systems.) Though it is unclear whether men or women are more accurately depicting the situation, many people are obviously ignorant about the reality of their partners' lives. And even if men are open to doing more at home so their wives can do more at work, the necessity may not occur to them. Gender equality could be boosted by some frank kitchen-table conversations.

How fracking boosts birth rates

The typical family in America is changing. Couples are increasingly reluctant to seal their relationships with the stamp of marriage, or to tie the knot before having children. In 1960 fewer than a tenth of births were to unmarried women, whereas these days around two-fifths of children are born out of wedlock. Economists wonder whether the changing economic fortunes of men might be driving these decisions, but struggle to disentangle the different factors at work. Recently, though, new evidence has emerged on the topic. Did, for example, the fracking boom affect family formation?

It seems plausible that someone might be reluctant to marry a person with poor or worsening economic prospects. And babies are expensive; to an economist, the idea that people might be more likely to have one when they get richer is a natural one. There is some historical evidence to support both hypotheses. In response to the Appalachian coal boom of the 1970s and 1980s, marriage rates went up, as did the share of babies born to married couples. More recently, a study by three economists, David Autor, David Dorn and Gordon Hanson, found that workers exposed to import competition from China during the 1990s and 2000s took a hit to their "marriage-market value". The negative shock seemed to turn people off marriage and children.

Another study, by Melissa Kearney and Riley Wilson, two economists at the University of Maryland, looks at the impact of the recent fracking boom in America, which boosted job opportunities for less-educated men. The economists wanted to see how this affected birth rates, both in and outside of marriage. They compared marriage and birth rates in areas where fracking had boosted the local economy with those where it had not had any effect. The researchers found no effect on marriage rates. But fertility rates did rise. On average, they found that $1,000 of extra fracking production per person was associated with an extra six births per 1,000 women.

The result confirms the hypothesis that better economic prospects lead to higher fertility. But it also sheds light on changing social attitudes in America: good times used to mean more wedding bells and babies, whereas now they just mean the latter. The policy prescriptions are not obvious. Whether or not people get married is their own business. But the finding does offer some comfort to those who worry that declining marriage rates are purely the product of worsening economic prospects for men. Clearly, some other factor is at play.

What explains Europe's low birth rates?

Julian Assange, the founder of WikiLeaks and apparently an amateur demographer, is worried about Europe's declining birth rate. In a tweet posted in 2017 he posited that "Capitalism + atheism + feminism = sterility = migration", and noted that the leaders of Britain, France, Germany and Italy were all childless. Never mind that Mr Assange needs a dictionary. "Sterility" means the inability to play a part in conception (often for medical reasons, or because a man has had a vasectomy or a woman has had her Fallopian tubes tied). What he presumably meant was childlessness, or perhaps a preference for fewer children – a preference, moreover, that until the advent of modern contraception women might hold but could not act on.

Mr Assange's tweet echoed sentiments expressed by RT (formerly Russia Today), a Kremlin-backed news organisation. Russian propagandists have long argued that the West's declining fertility rate is evidence of its decline. An RT editorial claimed that "Europe has been committing protracted demographic suicide for several decades". (Russia's own fertility rate stands at 1.8 births per woman, not much above the western European average of 1.6.) Critics responded sharply to Mr Assange's tweet, countering that a country's birth rate depends largely on how rich it is. But is there any germ of truth in what he said?

Birth rates are indeed highly correlated with national income: wealth is a powerful contraceptive, and this more than anything else explains Europe's low birth rates. But the fertility rates of many European countries are lower than would be expected if GDP per person were the only factor that mattered. Romania, for instance, has 1.5 births per adult woman. Based purely on its level of economic development, that figure would be expected to be around 2.1. What about the factors Mr Assange mentioned? Prosperity, capitalism, secularism and feminism all tend to be found in the same places. To try to distinguish the impact of each, *The Economist* tested their relationships with fertility rates across different countries.

Julian, unassuaged

The relationship between fertility and wealth

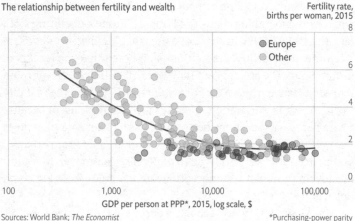

Fertility rate,
births per woman, 2015

- Europe
- Other

GDP per person at PPP*, 2015, log scale, $

Sources: World Bank; *The Economist*   *Purchasing-power parity

To measure religious observance, our data team used survey data
from the Pew Research Centre, a think-tank. Levels of capitalism
or feminism are harder to quantify, but an economic-liberty index
produced by the Heritage Foundation, another think-tank, and
a gender-equality index from the UN Development Programme
(UNDP) may serve as proxies.

Once GDP per person was taken into account, levels of capitalism,
thus measured, did nothing extra to explain variations in birth rates.
Both gender equality and the share of population that is irreligious
did seem to play a part. But while those two traits may help explain
why eastern European countries have far lower birth rates than
Middle Eastern and Latin American ones with similar levels of
income, neither was a meaningful predictor of fertility rates within
Europe. Birth rates in egalitarian and irreligious Scandinavia are
comparable to those in Catholic Italy, where women are expected
to care for both babies and older relatives. In short, variations in
enthusiasm for capitalism and feminism do not explain variations
in European birth rates, despite Mr Assange's suggestion. Countries
in eastern Europe and East Asia, moreover, tend to have both low

birth rates and negligible numbers of immigrants. So the last step in Mr Assange's equation, linking low birth rates to higher rates of migration, makes no sense at all.

Why America still allows child marriage

Child marriage is common in the developing world, where a third of girls, on average, marry before the age of 18. At that rate, another 1.2bn women will have got married as children by 2050. Almost all of the countries in the top 20 spots in a ranking of states with the highest rates of child marriage are African. Far less well-known is the prevalence of the practice in America – and almost always among girls. The country's diplomats are active in international efforts to ban child marriage abroad, but American children are still permitted to marry (albeit, usually, with parental consent and the approval of a judge or a clerk).

Child marriage is most common in America's conservative religious communities and poor, rural areas. But it can be found in all socio-economic strata and in secular, as well as pious, families. More than 207,000 American minors were married between 2000 and 2015, according to an investigation by *Frontline*, a television programme. Over two-thirds were 17 years old, but 985 were 14, and ten were just 12. Twenty-seven states have no minimum age for marriage. Encouragingly, the practice has become less common in recent years. This reflects changing social norms, higher rates of school attendance for girls and a decline in marriage generally. Whereas 23,500 minors got married in 2000, that figure had dropped to a little over 9,000 by 2010. Yet even as recently as 2014 more than 57,000 minors aged 15 to 17 were married. They entered perhaps the most important legal contract of their lives while, in most cases, not being considered legal adults. This means they cannot file for divorce, sign rental leases or seek protection in a shelter if they are abused.

Opponents of a ban on child marriage can be found across the political spectrum. Social conservatives argue that early marriages can reduce out-of-wedlock births as well as the number of single mothers on welfare. They also want to see religious traditions and customs protected. Libertarians say that marriage should be a choice made apart from the state. On the left, the American Civil

Liberties Union and Planned Parenthood, a national group that offers reproductive-health services, have defended the practice because banning it would intrude on the right to marry. Supporters of a ban hold that if children are seriously committed to each other, they can wait until they are 18 to marry. They also argue that religious customs that hurt children should not be protected.

Parents may think they have their child's best interest in mind by allowing an early marriage, especially if their daughter is pregnant. But in the vast majority of cases they actually harm her, sometimes irreparably. Between 70 and 80% of child marriages end in divorce. Married children are twice as likely to live in poverty and three times more likely to be beaten by spouses than married adults are. Around 50% more of them drop out of high school, and they are four times less likely to finish college. They are at considerably higher risk of diabetes, cancer, stroke and other physical illnesses. And they are much more likely to suffer from mental-health problems. That is why activists are so intransigent in pushing for a complete ban. And they are gaining ground. Virginia, Texas and New York have introduced laws that restrict marriage to legal adults. (In some states, people under 18 can become legal adults, with the associated rights, in order to marry.) Connecticut has banned marriage for under-16s. In 11 other states legislation restricting child marriage is in the pipeline; Arizona, Florida, Maryland, Massachusetts, New Jersey and Pennsylvania are considering blanket bans on marriage for those under 18. But no American state has passed a law that categorically forbids the practice.

Also on the menu: oddities of food and drink

The surprising link between avocados and crime

In English the word "avocado" refers to a fleshy fruit, native to Mexico. In Spanish an *abogado* is a lawyer. That is apt. The avocado has found itself flirting with the law on numerous occasions in recent years. What is the link between avocados and crime?

Since the late 1990s the world's appetite for avocados has steadily increased. In 2013 global production reached 4.7m metric tonnes – twice the level in 1998. A few factors explain the boom. Clever marketing has drawn consumers to the fruit for its high nutritional content (it is full of the sort of "good" fats lauded by dieticians) and health benefits, such as lowering the risk of heart disease. Moreover, it is also the main component in guacamole, a dip that has benefited from the rising popularity of Mexican fast food, such as tacos. As a result, traditional markets have expanded while new ones have emerged: China's avocado imports quadrupled in the five years from 2008.

But sometimes there are not enough avocados to go round. In 2016 bad weather in New Zealand and Australia brought harvesting to a halt. Bush fires destroyed orchards while heavy rainfall delayed picking of the fruit. Prices in New Zealand hit NZ$4.61 ($3.25) per avocado in June that year, the highest since records began in 1966. This prompted some people to take the law into their own hands, pilfering large quantities of the fruit from avocado orchards and selling them on the black market. High prices in 2017 led to another spate of night-time raids on orchards. And in May 2018 average prices hit a new high of NZ$5.06, prompting some restaurants to remove avocados from their menus. In Mexico, meanwhile, which accounts for around one-third of global avocado production, the crime is of an altogether different sort. The country is by far the biggest exporter of the fruit – and plans to stay that way. Growers there (or at least the cartels that control them) have taken to cutting down forests illegally to make way for more extensive farming. In Costa Rica, a ban on imports of Hass, a kind of avocado, led to smuggling of the fruit across the border from Panama.

Boosting production quickly is hard, because the avocado is a difficult plant to grow. As with harvests occurring at different times in different countries, there can be sudden swings in availability and price. (Poor harvests in Mexico, California and Peru caused prices to spike in 2017.) As long as demand exceeds supply and avocados remain a lucrative product, dodgy dealing is likely to continue. Tweets declaring the avocado to be "#overcado" seem to have done little to dampen enthusiasm for the fruit. Those new to its appeal are unlikely to relinquish the green stuff anytime soon.

Why China's dog-meat market has expanded

Every year during the summer solstice, a dog-eating festival takes place in Yulin, a city in the southern Chinese province of Guangxi. It always sparks controversy, as photographs of dogs being fried or treated cruelly go viral. In 2017, animal-rights activists and American congressmen demanded that China ban the eating of dogs and cats, as Taiwan did earlier that year. Yulin's local government took modest steps to restrain or hide some of the more contentious activities, such as selling dogs in food markets. Still, the festival was packed. Why has the controversial culinary habit become so popular in China?

Contrary to cliché, dog meat has not always been a common item in the Chinese diet. Unlike in the West, eating dogs has never been taboo, but it appears to have been rare in the past. Government accounts single out butchers who sold dog meat, suggesting it was unusual and worthy of record. According to Guo Peng of Shandong University, one of the few people to have studied the dog-meat market, only China's ethnic Korean minority eat dog with regularity. The majority Han population, she argues, see it as a medicinal food, which is believed to warm the body in winter or cool it in summer – hence the timing of the Yulin festival at the mid-year solstice, literally the dog days of summer. Traditionally, Ms Guo says, most people have only eaten dog once a year, if at all. According to a survey conducted in 2016 by Dataway Horizon, a polling firm, and Capital Animal Welfare Association, a Chinese NGO, almost 70% of Chinese people say they have never eaten dog. Of those who have, most claim they did so by accident – when invited to a social or business dinner, for example.

So why is the Yulin festival packed? And why do restaurants in many cities proudly put dog on the menu? The one-word answer is: criminality. Dog meat, a bit like drugs, has become a lucrative source of criminal income. For the past decade Ms Guo has been going from village to village in Shandong province, on the east coast, asking inhabitants what has been happening to their animals. In one, villagers told her that a third of their dogs had been stolen between 2007 and 2011. Hunters, she discovered, have been roaming the countryside in vans, killing dogs with poisoned darts and selling them on to middlemen. Hunters got about 10 yuan ($1.30) for a kilogram of meat, so a medium-sized dog might be worth 70–80 yuan. One young man she interviewed was hunting so he could earn enough to get married. Hunted dog meat has increased the supply and reduced prices, boosting the size of the overall market. Ms Guo thinks Shandong and neighbouring Henan now supply a significant portion of China's dog-meat business.

In a way, the dog-meat trade exploits the fact that modernisation in these provinces is incomplete. In villages, dogs are still guardians. In big cities, they are increasingly becoming pets. The number of dogs registered as pets in Beijing, for example, has been growing by 25% a year for a decade. It now stands at about 2m, more than in New York. Concern for animal welfare has been growing in parallel, indicated by an increase in animal hospitals, animal-rescue and adoption agencies, and changing attitudes. Animal-welfare concerns are coming more into conflict with dog hunters and dog-meat eaters. Eventually they will probably snuff out the trade.

Why obesity is a growing problem in poor countries

When people think of nutritional woes in the developing world, they probably think of famine. But the number of young people in low- and middle-income countries who are obese is catching up with the number who are underweight. In 1975 obese children were almost unknown outside the rich world: just 0.3% of people in developing countries aged five to 19 had a body-mass index (BMI) more than two standard deviations above the average for their age and gender, the World Health Organisation's definition of obesity. That figure has soared to 7% today. Meanwhile, the proportion of children who are underweight (with a BMI two standard deviations below average for their age and gender) in low- and middle-income countries has declined, from 13% to 10%. According to the WHO, if current trends continue, the number of obese children worldwide will surpass that of the undernourished by 2022.

It might seem paradoxical that countries can have high levels both of hunger and of obesity. But the two are linked. Poor parents tend to seek the most affordable meals they can find to fill up their children. Thanks to the spread of convenience foods and energy-dense processed carbohydrates, the cheapest foods often deliver precious few nutrients relative to the calories they contain, putting children who eat a lot of them on a fast track to obesity.

As a result, countries where the number of underweight children falls sharply often overshoot in the other direction. South Africa, for example, slashed the share of its youngsters who are underweight from about 20% in 1975 to less than 5% today. Over the same period, its childhood obesity rate went from roughly zero to more than 10%. Similarly, in China, the proportion of underweight youngsters fell from 6% to 3%, but its obesity rate likewise grew from almost nothing to over 10%. In 1975 fewer than half a million young Chinese were obese; now nearly 28m are.

Childhood obesity raises the risk of all sorts of maladies later in life – particularly diabetes, which now causes more deaths

Young-aged spread

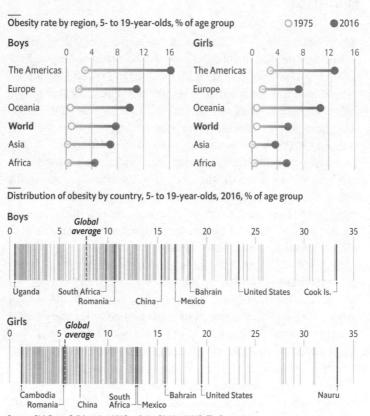

Obesity rate by region, 5- to 19-year-olds, % of age group   ○ 1975 ● 2016

Boys

	0	4	8	12	16
The Americas					
Europe					
Oceania					
World					
Asia					
Africa					

Girls

	0	4	8	12	16
The Americas					
Europe					
Oceania					
World					
Asia					
Africa					

Distribution of obesity by country, 5- to 19-year-olds, 2016, % of age group

Boys

Uganda   South Africa   Romania   China   Mexico   Bahrain   United States   Cook Is.

Global average

Girls

Cambodia   Romania   China   South Africa   Mexico   Bahrain   United States   Nauru

Global average

Sources: Risk Factor Collaboration; UN Population Division; WHO; *The Economist*

than AIDS, tuberculosis and malaria combined. Governments in countries where underweight children are still common would be well-advised to help families obtain food that will not simply replace one nutritional problem with another.

The Argentine–American lemon war of 2001–2018

In May 2018 America received its first shipment of Argentine lemons in 17 years, following the lifting of an import ban imposed by the Department of Agriculture in 2001. The resulting export squeeze had seen relations sour between the countries, as Donald Trump observed: "One of the reasons he's here is about lemons. And I'll tell him about North Korea, and he'll tell me about lemons," he said when Mauricio Macri, the Argentine leader, visited him in April 2017. A resolution to the citrus wars was keenly awaited. America, which is the world's largest consumer of the fruit, can now source lemons from the fourth-largest producer. What prompted the original dispute, and why did peace break out at last?

The dispute had deep roots. For most of the 20th century, imports of Argentine lemons were restricted under quarantine rules, for fear that the fruit might bring in pests that could hurt American crops. When a relaxation was proposed in 2000, a consortium of growers in California and Arizona – which account for all of America's domestic production – sued the agency responsible for protecting America's plants and animals. Citrus fruits, they argued, had become a bargaining chip in America's desire to open Argentina to its exports; in their view the risk of contamination remained. The courts sided with the farmers, and the ban was reinstated in 2001. In the years that followed, lukewarm relations between the two countries did not help. Nor did export taxes imposed on producers by an Argentine government trying to shore up its disastrous finances. The quarrel went to the WTO in 2012, as part of a bilateral tit-for-tat dispute involving meat and other foodstuffs.

Mr Macri, elected president in 2015 on a pro-market mandate, eliminated most taxes on agricultural exports. His arrival also prompted a rapprochement with the United States. After Barack Obama visited the Argentine capital in March 2016, American officials travelled to the country to inspect citrus orchards, prompting the outgoing Obama administration to say in December

2016 that it would lift the ban. Mr Trump's inauguration a few weeks later – and his threats to withdraw from the North American Free Trade Agreement – led Argentina to worry that the measure would be indefinitely delayed, after an initial 60-day stay on the decision was renewed by the new administration in March 2017. Mr Macri's visit cleared the way for imports to resume in May 2017, but American growers once again mounted a legal challenge against the decision, arguing that it had been made for political rather than scientific reasons.

Mr Trump's conspiracy-minded critics suggested, for example, that allowing imports was payback for California's strong support for Hillary Clinton in the 2016 elections. That was probably reading too much into it. In March 2018 a judge rejected the citrus-growers' argument, allowing imports to resume the following month. The president's most substantial justification for supporting an end to the ban was that "the lemon business is big, big business". His support for imports was hardly sign of a deeply felt belief in trade liberalisation, in short. Even for advocates of free trade, the resolution of this dispute left a bitter aftertaste.

Which European country has the most craft breweries per person?

These are not vintage times for Europe's brewers. Overall beer sales have been fairly flat for years, at around 375m hectolitres per year. Since 2012 consumption per person has fallen slightly in most of the biggest beer-drinking countries. But beneath this seemingly uneventful surface, change is brewing: smaller producers and craft breweries have been gaining market share at the expense of established brands. Between 2010 and 2016 the number of microbrewing businesses in Europe nearly tripled, surpassing the 7,000 mark for the first time.

Small-scale brewing owes its success to several factors. Richer consumers are increasingly turning to more distinctive, local products rather than mass-market brands. Microbreweries are relatively cheap and easy to establish: they can be housed in industrial estates, old factories, farm sheds and even campsites. Many small brewers are keen to open their workplaces to help educate the more discerning drinker. This trend is particularly

Wort is going on?

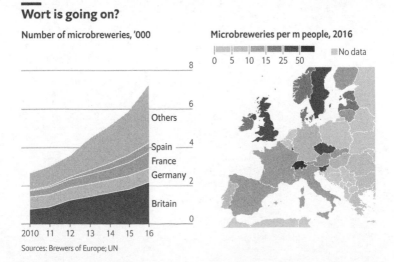

Number of microbreweries, '000

Others
Spain
France
Germany
Britain

2010 11 12 13 14 15 16

Microbreweries per m people, 2016

0 5 10 15 25 50 ▪ No data

Sources: Brewers of Europe; UN

prevalent in Britain, which is home to 2,200 microbreweries all by itself. Tours range from the two small units occupied by the Padstow Brewery, located in a fashionable Cornish resort, to Meantime, a larger establishment in Greenwich now owned by Japan's Asahi. Festivals and the stocking by pubs of locally brewed beers have further spread the word.

The shift towards smaller brewers shows no sign of abating. Forecasts for the craft industry look stout, with Technavio, a market-research firm, projecting that revenues will grow by around 10% a year until 2021. To keep pace with demand and stand out from the growing crowd, microbrewers will need to continue devising ever more inventive names, and striking packing designs, for their artisanal ales. Stand still, and the likes of Born Hoppy, Yeastie Boys and the 4 Hopmen of the Apocalypse will no longer be the Cream of the Crop.

Why some American cities don't like food trucks

When gourmet food trucks first appeared on America's streets in 2008, many dismissed them as a fad. A decade later it is clear that the trendy trucks – known for offbeat dishes, low prices and clever use of social media – are here to stay. That does not mean they are always welcome. In recent years many cities have passed laws restricting where and when food trucks can operate. But regulating the mobile-food industry has proved difficult. How do cities keep food trucks off their streets?

The food-truck revolution is often credited to Roy Choi, who began selling $2 Korean barbecue tacos on the streets of Los Angeles in 2008. By 2015 America could boast more than 4,000 food trucks, which together were bringing in some $1.2bn per year. Not everyone finds them an appetising prospect, however. Critics say food trucks block streets, take up valuable parking spaces and disrupt pavements with crowds, waste and noise. Restaurant owners complain that because mobile vendors do not have to pay rent or property taxes, they enjoy an unfair advantage. Lawmakers have responded to these complaints with stricter regulation. In 2011 Boston set aside public sites where food trucks could do business – and barred them from operating elsewhere in the city.

In 2013, Washington DC passed a similar law, delimiting "zones" where food trucks could operate legally. In cities that do allow food trucks to ply the public streets, truck owners typically face limits on how long they are allowed to park in a single place. In Denver vendors are given four hours per spot. In other cities, limits can be as short as 30 minutes. Some cities have gone further, imposing minimum distances between food trucks and existing bricks-and-mortar businesses. In Baltimore trucks may not set up shop within 300 feet of a restaurant. In some cities, these "buffer zones" can have a radius as large as 500 feet.

Such regulation has stifled the food-truck industry in some of America's biggest cities. In New York, where vendors have to shell out as much as $25,000 to rent a permit on the black market (the city has not increased the number of licences in three decades), and may not park in any of the city's 85,000 metered parking spaces, launching a new food truck has become nearly impossible. In Chicago, where truck owners cannot operate within 200 feet of bricks-and-mortar restaurants and must carry GPS devices to verify their whereabouts, the food-truck market has stalled. Despite being home to more than 7,300 restaurants and 144 craft breweries, Chicago has just 70 licensed food trucks. But some are fighting the regulations: in 2011 the Institute for Justice, a libertarian law firm, successfully challenged an El Paso law that prohibited food trucks from operating within 1,000 feet of any existing restaurant. In 2015 the group won a similar case against San Antonio, which had a longstanding 300-foot rule. Where there is a wheel (or four), there is a way.

How wine glasses have got bigger over the years

In 1674 George Ravenscroft, an English glass merchant, was granted a patent for the discovery, made at his factory in London, that adding lead oxide to molten glass resulted in a clearer, more durable product. Thus was born lead crystal, and with it the fashion, in England, of drinking wine from glass vessels rather than, say, pewter ones. Wine glasses have evolved since then, of course, and one aspect of this evolution is of particular interest to Theresa Marteau and her colleagues from the Behaviour and Health Research Unit at Cambridge University. Dr Marteau suspected that glasses have got bigger over the years, and that this may have contributed to the increased drinking of wine in Britain – an increase that has been particularly marked in recent decades.

She and her team obtained data on glass volumes going back to about 1700, from sources including the Royal Household (which buys a new set for each monarch) and the Ashmolean, the university museum of Cambridge's arch-rival, Oxford. Altogether, they recorded the capacity of 411 glasses and, as the chart shows, there has indeed been a near-continuous tendency for that capacity to increase since Ravenscroft's day (he died in 1683). There was also a notable acceleration of the process starting in about 1990. In all, the average capacity of a wine glass increased from 66ml in the 1700s to almost 450ml in 2017.

That this volumetric inflation has stimulated wine consumption – Dr Marteau's second hypothesis – is hard to prove. But it may have done. The amount of wine drunk in Britain has risen more than sevenfold since 1960, while the population has grown by only 25%. Data collected between 1978 and 2005 by Britain's Office of National Statistics (ONS) suggest the proportion of adults drinking wine fell from 60% to 50% over that period, while the average weekly consumption of wine drinkers tripled, when measured as units of alcohol. Another data set, collected by the Institute of Alcohol Studies, a temperance charity, suggests that the amount of alcohol from all sources (measured as pure ethanol) consumed per head in

Bottoms up

Capacity of wine glasses in England, ml; 1700–2016

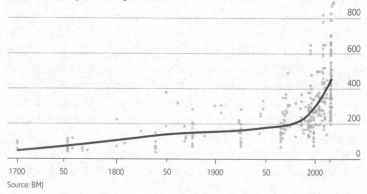

Source: BMJ

Britain is about the same as it was in 1980, though it has fluctuated quite a bit in the intervening years, peaking in 2004.

Meanwhile, work designed to test directly the idea that glass size matters, which Dr Marteau published in 2016, produced mixed results. She looked at the consequences for wine sales at a bar in Cambridge of serving its wares in both bigger and smaller glasses than normal, while keeping the serving sizes on offer (125ml or 175ml, according to customer choice) the same. In weeks when the bigger glasses were used, wine sales went up by 9% on average. The larger vessels, it seemed, were indeed encouraging customers to order refills more often. On the other hand, in weeks when the size of the glasses was below normal, sales did not go down. Reducing glass sizes, then, does not keep people sober.

Why food packaging is good for the environment

Supermarkets encourage shoppers to buy products using clever layouts and cunning promotions. Alluring packaging helps too, while also keeping food clean and safe to eat. Green types balk at plastic-encased bananas. But some forms of packaging, especially for meat, can be an environmental boon. A third of food is wasted between field and plate, according to the UN, costing billions of dollars every year. Global greenhouse-gas emissions associated with food waste are higher than those of India, because chucking out items means the water, fuel, fertiliser and other inputs that went into them are wasted too. Such harm to the planet can be reduced if the length of time that food lingers on shelves or in fridges can be extended. This is especially true for meat.

Meat provides 17% of mankind's global calorific intake, but it is costly in terms of both cash and resources, requiring a disproportionate amount of water and feed. More land is given over to grazing animals than for any other single purpose. Overall, the livestock sector accounts for as much pollution as is spewed out by all the world's vehicles. Ruminant livestock, such as cattle and sheep, have stomachs containing bacteria able to digest tough, cellulose-rich plants. But along the way, huge volumes of methane are belched too – a greenhouse gas more than 20 times as powerful as carbon dioxide over the span of a century.

Wrapping meat in vacuum packaging prevents oxidation, extending its lifespan. It allows meat to stay on shelves for between five and eight days, rather than two to four when simply wrapped on a polystyrene tray or draped behind a counter. This pleases big grocery chains, which stand to save thousands of dollars a week if less meat has to be either marked down or thrown out. It also delights consumers, as vacuum-packed meat is more tender.

But doesn't packaging itself require resources to produce? Yes, but the emissions from creating it are less than those associated with food waste. According to estimates, for every tonne of packaging, the equivalent of between one and two tonnes of carbon dioxide is released. For every tonne of food wasted, the equivalent of more than three tonnes of carbon dioxide is emitted. So although supermarkets have been focusing on curbing the amount of packaging they use, many now consider extending shelf life the most important environmental consideration. Given that meat consumption is expected to grow by 75% by the middle of the century, vacuum packaging offers an important way to boost resource efficiency and access to an important protein source.

Peak booze? Alcohol consumption is falling around the world

The world appears to have passed peak booze. The volume of alcoholic drinks consumed globally fell by 1.4% in 2016, to 250bn litres, according to IWSR, a research firm. It was the second consecutive year of decline, and only the third since data started to be collected in 1994. The main cause of the drop-off is that people are drinking less beer, which accounts for three-quarters of all alcohol drunk by volume. Worldwide beer consumption shrank by 1.8% to 185bn litres in 2016. Yet because the drinking-age population of the world grew by 1% in that time, beer consumption per drinking-age adult declined even more, by 3.2%. The overall drop is almost entirely because of declines in three of the five biggest markets. China, Brazil and Russia accounted for 99.6% of the global reduction in the volume of beer drunk in 2016.

Both economics and changing tastes play a part. China overtook America to become the world's biggest market for beer (by volume, not value) in 2001. It now quaffs a quarter of all beer.

Drying up
Global alcohol consumption

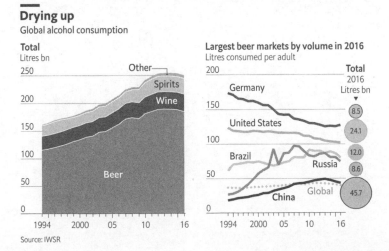

Source: IWSR

But consumption per person peaked in 2013 and dropped further in 2016. Beer's appeal is waning among older drinkers, with over-30s moving to wine and over-40s favouring *baijiu*, the national spirit. Elsewhere, recessions have hit beer-drinkers' pockets. In both Brazil and Russia, consumption by the average adult fell by 7%.

Beer-drinking patterns also change as countries grow richer. In a study published in 2016, Liesbeth Colen and Johan Swinnen of the University of Leuven examined the effects of income growth and globalisation on beer consumption in 80 countries between 1961 and 2009. They found that as GDP per person increased in poorer countries, beer became more popular. But when it reached around $27,000 per person, consumption began to fall: consumers may opt for more expensive drinks, such as wine, once they can afford them. And beer consumption rose as countries became more globalised, the authors found. As international drinks companies move in, punters may find a new favourite tipple. For all these reasons, consumers in emerging markets have driven beer sales ever upwards for decades. But now the IWSR's figures suggest that the froth is coming off the booze market.

Why wheat has a more complex genome than humans

The domestication of wheat and other staple crops in the Middle East some 10,000 years ago allowed for persistent settlement above a level of mere subsistence – and thus kicked off the rise of civilisation. Early farmers grew naturally occurring hybrids of wheat, and over time tamed them into a robust, easy-to-harvest and high-yielding species, the history of which is revealed in the genome of modern bread wheat. It is an enormously dense, complicated genome. And unlike the genetic codes of staples like rice, soya and maize, scientists struggled until 2017 to crack it. Why was it so hard to decipher – and was it worth the effort?

The genomes of ancient wheats, such as wild emmer, contain more DNA base pairs than human genomes do. Domesticated hybrids, like bread wheat, are even larger. The genome of bread wheat has nearly six times as many DNA base pairs as the human genome (about 17bn compared with humans' 3bn). That is in part because humans are diploid, with two sets of chromosomes, whereas the chromosomes of bread wheat come in sets of six (corresponding to the three ancient wheats of which bread wheat is a hybrid). Furthermore, the DNA of ancient wheat contained a huge amount of duplication. This means that bread wheat not only contains an enormous amount of genetic information, but that much of it is repeated. That makes decoding its genome complex. With fewer unique pieces, it is harder to fit the jigsaw together.

Other staple food crops had their genomes sequenced long before bread wheat. But they are much simpler: popular strains of maize, soya and rice have 2.3bn, 1.1bn and 420m DNA base pairs respectively. The breakthrough with bread wheat came in 2016, when several different academic and industry projects matured. Both the International Wheat Genome Sequencing Consortium (IWGSC), which includes wheat farmers, breeders and scientists, and an independent group led by Johns Hopkins University, managed to sequence it. Others decoded wild emmer, an ancestor of both bread and durum wheat, and *Aegilops tauschii*, another of bread wheat's ancestors.

Decoding wheat's genome is useful for two reasons. First, it makes it easier for researchers to manipulate wheat without recourse to so much trial and error. Second, it allows them to insert attractive traits from ancient wheats into modern ones, rather than introducing genes from other organisms altogether (a process known as transgenics). These ancient wheats may have better resistance to pests or better tolerance of drought, but offer poorer yields and quality, says Catherine Feuillet, head of trait research at Bayer, a German pharmaceuticals firm and an important player in IWGSC's gene project. Crossing an ancient wheat with a modern one would normally take a decade, but by using the genome as a sort of index of the wheat's positive traits, iteration and improvement can be done much faster. And with the genome to hand, and in the public domain (the IWGSC is eschewing patents), more researchers can get involved. Help may even come from unexpected corners. Ms Feuillet talks of finding "a high-school student who may finally be able to find a key resistance gene for a fungal disease".

Asian countries are eating more wheat

So central is rice to life in Asia that in many countries, rather than asking "how are you?" people ask, "have you eaten rice yet?" Around 90% of the world's rice is consumed in Asia – 60% of it in China, India and Indonesia alone. In every large country except Pakistan, Asians eat more rice than the global average. Between the early 1960s and the early 1990s, rice consumption per head rose steadily, from an average of 85kg per year to 103kg. As Asia grew wealthier, people began to consume more food, and rice was available and affordable.

But rice consumption is now more-or-less flat in Asia as a whole. And in Asia's better-off countries rice is going out of fashion. Figures from the United States Department of Agriculture (USDA) suggest that rice consumption per head has fallen since 2000 in

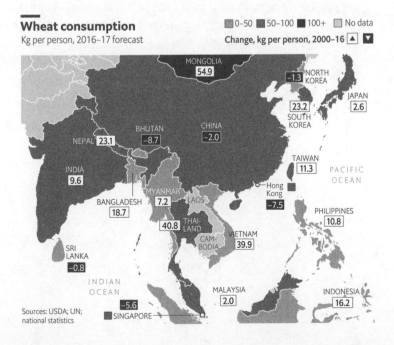

Wheat consumption
Kg per person, 2016–17 forecast

■ 0–50 ■ 50–100 ■ 100+ □ No data
Change, kg per person, 2000–16 ▲ ▼

Sources: USDA; UN; national statistics

China, Indonesia and South Korea, and has crashed in Singapore. Asians are following a rule known as Bennett's law, which states that as people become wealthier they get more of their calories from vegetables, fruit, meat, fish and dairy products. At the same time, many of them are starting to replace the rice in their diets with wheat.

Wheat consumption is rising quickly in countries like Thailand and Vietnam. South-East Asian countries consumed 23.4m tonnes of wheat in 2016–17, estimates the USDA – up from 16.5m tonnes in 2012–13. Almost all of it was imported. In South Asia consumption is estimated to have grown from 121m to 139m tonnes over the same period.

This trend has a long way to run, predicts Rabobank, a bank. South-East Asians still eat only 26kg of wheat a year, much less than the world average of 78kg. They seem unperturbed by price rises: wheat-eating kept growing even as the grain became more expensive between 2009 and 2013. Still, rice will remain central to many Asian cultures. People are unlikely to start greeting each other by asking if they have eaten bagels just yet.

By the numbers: economical, with the truth

The easiest way to get rich in America

Americans are admirably optimistic about their ability to shape their own future. One survey found that nearly three-quarters of Americans thought hard work was a "very important" component of success, while just 62% put it down to a good education and less than a fifth to inherited wealth. But the United States ranks poorly compared with other advanced economies when it comes to income inequality and social mobility. So what must an ambitious young American do to get rich?

A new study by Raj Chetty of Stanford University and a collective of other economists helps answer this question. By matching data from the Department of Education with 30m tax returns, Mr Chetty and his colleagues have constructed a data set that reveals to researchers both the income distributions of graduates of particular colleges, and how incomes vary depending on how rich the graduates' parents were. The data show that attending an elite college is a good way of securing an upper-middle-class lifestyle: graduates of Ivy League-calibre universities have roughly the same chance of breaking into the top 20% of the income distribution, regardless of family background. Paths to the upper-middle class exist for those who graduate from lesser-known universities too, because earnings depend even more on what one studies than where. On average, graduates of lesser-known engineering colleges such as Kettering University and the Stevens Institute of Technology do just as well as those from the Ivy League.

But a good education alone cannot propel the merely upper-middle class into the ranks of the rich. Few engineers, nurses or pharmacists make it to the top 1%, which is dominated by bankers and other financiers. Recruiters in the financial industry place high premiums on pedigree. Here the Ivies play an outsize role; graduates of elite private universities such as Harvard and Yale are much more likely to end up on Wall Street. Moreover, data from Mr Chetty and colleagues show that it helps to start off rich in the first place.

This trend is even more pronounced at the very top of the income distribution. Between 1999 and 2004, just 2% of Princetonians came from the families in the lowest 20% of earnings, while 3.2% came from families in the top 0.1%. The admissions process at top colleges is sometimes further skewed by the preferential treatment given to family members of alumni. When the researchers looked at Harvard's most recently admitted class, they found that 27% had a relative who also went to that "college near Boston". This suggests that the simplest way to become extremely rich is by being born to rich parents. The second-easiest way is to find a rich spouse. If neither approach works, you could try to get into a top college – but remember that not all Princetonians become plutocrats.

Why women still earn much less than men

Payroll clerks across Britain have been busier than usual. New rules mean that, as of April 2018, all large employers are required to publish annual data on the gap in pay between their male and female workers. In America, by contrast, President Donald Trump halted a similar rule that would have taken effect the same year. Such requirements are meant to energise efforts towards equal pay for men and women. The data suggest that a new approach is needed. In the OECD, a club of mostly rich countries, median wages for women working full time are 85% of those for men. Why do women still earn so much less?

Contrary to popular belief, it is not because employers pay women less than men for doing the same jobs. According to data from 25 countries, gathered by Korn Ferry, a consultancy, women earn 98% of the wages of men who are in the same roles at the same employers. Instead, the gap arises because women outnumber men in lower-paid jobs, such as secretarial and administrative roles, whereas men predominate in senior positions. That means that in a typical company, average male pay is higher than average female pay. Women also cluster in occupations and industries that pay lower salaries overall. Primary-school teachers in the OECD, for example, earn nearly 20% less than the average for university graduates. In the European Union nearly 70% of working women are in occupations where at least 60% of employees are female. In America, the four jobs done by the biggest numbers of women – teacher, nurse, secretary and health-care assistant – are all at least 80% female.

The main reason why women are less likely than men to reach higher-level positions is that they are their children's primary carers. In eight countries polled by *The Economist* and YouGov in 2017, between 44% and 75% of women with children living at home said they had scaled back at work after becoming mothers – either by working fewer hours or by switching to a less demanding job, such as one requiring less travel or overtime. Only 13–37% of fathers said they had done so, and more than half of those men said their partner had also scaled back. This pattern means that men get a better shot at a pay rise or a promotion than their female colleagues, and are less likely to work in jobs for which they are overqualified. One study estimated that in America, women's future wages fall, on average, by 4% per child, and by 10% per child in the case of the highest-earning, most skilled white women. In Britain, a mother's wages fall by 2% for each year she is out of the workforce, and by twice as much if she has good school-leaving qualifications.

Women's lower salaries mean that they often fall into poverty when they divorce or are widowed. Lack of financial independence prevents some from leaving abusive partners. Policies and workplace norms that make it easier for men to split parental duties equally with their partners can help. Parents, for their part, need to instil in their children the idea that they can be anything – and not only if they are girls. Gender equality will remain elusive until boys are as excited as girls about becoming teachers, nurses and full-time parents.

Why China is rebuilding the old Silk Road

In May 2017 Xi Jinping welcomed 28 heads of state and government to Beijing for a coming-out party to celebrate the "belt and road" initiative, his most ambitious foreign-policy project. Launched in 2013 as "one belt, one road", it involves China underwriting billions of dollars of infrastructure investment in countries along the old Silk Road linking it with Europe. The ambition is immense. China is spending roughly $150bn a year in the 68 countries that have signed up to the scheme. The summit meeting (called a forum) attracted the largest number of foreign dignitaries to Beijing since the Olympic Games in 2008. Yet few European leaders showed up. For the most part they have ignored the implications of China's initiative. What are those implications, and is the West right to be sanguine?

The project is the clearest expression so far of Mr Xi's determination to break with Deng Xiaoping's dictum to "hide our capabilities and bide our time; never try to take the lead". The Belt and Road Forum (with its unfortunate acronym, BARF) was the second set-piece event in 2017 at which Mr Xi laid out China's claim to global leadership. (The first was a speech against protectionism made at the World Economic Forum in Davos in January.) In 2014, Wang Yi, the foreign minister, said the initiative was the most important component of Mr Xi's foreign policy. Its ultimate aim is to make Eurasia (dominated by China) an economic and trading area to rival the transatlantic one (dominated by America).

Behind this broad strategic imperative lies a plethora of secondary motivations – the number and variety of which prompt Western scepticism about the coherence and practicality of the project. By investing in infrastructure, Mr Xi hopes to find a more profitable home for China's vast foreign-exchange reserves, most of which are in low-interest-bearing American government securities. He also hopes to create new markets for Chinese companies, such as high-speed rail firms, and to export some of his country's vast excess capacity in cement, steel and other metals. By investing in volatile countries in central Asia, he reckons he can create a more stable neighbourhood for China's own restive western provinces of Xinjiang and Tibet. And by encouraging more Chinese projects around the South China Sea, the initiative could bolster China's claims in that area (the "road" in "belt and road" refers to sea lanes). Yet some of these ambitions contradict others: is a dodgy project in central Asia a better place to invest than American government securities? And with different motivations go conflicting interests. There is infighting between the most important Chinese institutions involved, including the ministry of commerce, the foreign ministry, the planning commission and China's provinces. To make matters worse, China is finding it hard to identify profitable projects in many belt-and-road countries (business people in China call it "One Road, One Trap"). To cap it all, China is facing a backlash against some of its plans, with elected governments in Sri Lanka and Myanmar repudiating or seeking to renegotiate projects approved by their authoritarian predecessors.

That may seem to justify Europeans' decision to stay away. But the suspicion that the project will fail could be misguided. Mr Xi needs the initiative because he has invested so much in it. China needs it because it provides an answer of sorts to some of its economic problems. And Asia needs it because of an insatiable thirst for infrastructure. The belt-and-road initiative has plenty of problems, but Mr Xi is determined to push ahead with it.

Why "death taxes" have fallen out of favour

Once they were feared. Only a few decades ago inheritance taxes and estate taxes took a big bite out of the largest fortunes when their owners passed on. Before the second world war Britons were more likely to pay inheritance tax on death than they were to pay income tax while living. Around the same time the top rate of estate tax in America was 77%. How things have changed: America could be on the verge of eliminating its estate tax entirely, while Britain is cutting the number of people who are subject to the tax each year by a third. A raft of countries, from India to Norway to Australia, have eliminated their inheritance taxes entirely. Why have governments all over the world turned away from death duties?

The economic argument in favour of cutting death duties is weaker than you might suspect. There is little evidence that lower death duties encourage saving or investment; nor does the prospect of being able to pass more on to their offspring encourage people to work harder. Instead, research suggests that a large proportion of bequests from one generation to the next are "accidental". People save money not to pass on, but to cover unexpected costs while they are alive. Nor is there much evidence that high death duties prompt rich folk to flee to lower-tax jurisdictions, which was one of the main arguments used in Sweden to justify its abolition of inheritance tax in 2004.

Perhaps a better explanation for why governments have turned against death duties is simply that the public hates them. Inheritances are deeply personal, and are often the biggest single gift that many give to causes they believe in or to loved ones they cherished. Many see the estate tax as a "double tax", since it is often paid on income that has already been subject to income tax. This is not the strongest of arguments, though. If avoiding double taxation were a requirement of good policy, then governments would also need to abolish sales taxes. Nonetheless, politicians have realised that they are onto a winner. Both George W. Bush and Donald Trump found, as presidential candidates, that promises to repeal the estate tax proved highly popular.

Yet some economists worry about the trend towards tiny or even zero death duties. The rich world has high levels of wealth inequality. Half of Europe's billionaires inherited their wealth, for instance. The annual flow of inheritances in some rich countries is around 10% of GDP, far above its level a few decades ago. If governments want to avoid the creation of a hereditary elite, they might want to think again about doing away with death duties.

Wealth inequality has been increasing since the stone age

The one-percenters are now gobbling up more of the economic pie in America – that much is well known. This trend, though disconcerting, is not unique to the modern era. A study by Timothy Kohler of Washington State University and 17 others found that inequality may well have been rising for several thousand years, at least in some parts of the world. The scholars examined 63 archaeological sites and estimated the levels of wealth inequality in the societies whose remains were dug up, by studying the distributions of house sizes.

As a measure they used the Gini coefficient (a perfectly equal society would have a Gini coefficient of zero; a society where one person owns all the wealth would have a coefficient of one). It rose from about 0.2 around 8000BC in Jerf el-Ahmar, on the Euphrates in modern-day Syria, to 0.5 in around 79AD in Pompeii. Data on burial goods, though sparse, suggest similar trends.

The researchers suggest agriculture is to blame. The nomadic

Nice digs

Gini coefficient of house sizes at archaeological sites
1=perfect inequality, 0=perfect equality

Source: "Greater post-Neolithic wealth disparities in Eurasia than in North America and Mesoamerica" by Timothy A. Kohler et al

lifestyle is not conducive to wealth accumulation: there is a limit to how much you can carry around. Only when humans switched to a settled existence based on farming did people truly begin to acquire material riches. Inequality rose steadily after the shift to agriculture, but tailed off in the Americas after around 2,500 years. In the old world, however, wealth inequality continued to climb for several millennia. That may be because Eurasia was richer in large mammals that could be domesticated. Horses and oxen greatly improved farm productivity – but livestock were mainly owned by the rich (who could also rent them out). In traditional African societies, livestock remain an important store of value. The agricultural revolution was good for humanity, because it supported a larger population and paved the way for modern civilisation. But it was awful for egalitarians.

What makes something a commodity?

A commodity, said Karl Marx, "appears at first sight an extremely obvious, trivial thing. But its analysis brings out that it is a very strange thing, abounding in metaphysical subtleties and theological niceties." A commodities trader might snort at such a definition: there is nothing much metaphysical, after all, about pork bellies, say, however divine (or sinful) the taste of bacon. Yet for thousands of years, from rice in China to gold, frankincense and myrrh in Biblical times, to spices in the days of empire, commodities have been the building blocks of commerce. At the peak of the China-led super-cycle in 2011, they accounted for one-third of the world's merchandise trade. They encompass an array of materials – from food and flowers to fossil fuels and metals – that appear to bear little relation to each other. What makes something a commodity?

In society at large, the word gets pretty bad press. In business-school jargon, commoditisation, of everything from silicon chips to Christmas cards, is associated with dull, repetitive products, however useful, that generate low margins. The extraction of physical commodities such as oil or iron ore, meanwhile, has an unseemly air to it. People talk of the "resource curse" (the impact of cyclical ups and downs in prices on poor countries), "Dutch disease" (the impact of high prices on exchange rates), and "blood oil" and "blood diamonds" (the use of proceeds from extractive industries to fund conflict). Some worry that even love has been commoditised by dating apps and websites.

In economic terms, commodities are vital components of commerce that are standardised and hence easy to exchange for goods of the same type, have a fairly uniform price around the world (excluding transport costs and taxes) and are used to make other products. They are extracted, grown and sold in sufficient quantities to be traded in highly liquid markets, often with futures and options to help producers and consumers protect themselves against price swings. Such commodities include cocoa and coffee, zinc and copper, wheat and soyabeans, silver and gold, and oil and coal, along with numerous other raw materials. Our lives, literally, depend on them. So do many of the world's economies – and not just corrupt petro-state dictatorships. Britain's industrial revolution would not have got going without coal.

Some raw materials would benefit from being treated like commodities, but are not. Diamonds do not qualify, because each one differs in quality. Rare-earth elements, though not as rare as the name suggests, are sold in differing grades, often via murky backroom deals, and the volumes are too low for a commodities exchange. Unlike oil, natural gas is not traded worldwide. Its price is mostly determined by long-term contracts that vary from region to region. It may, however, be next in line to join the ranks of global commodities, as growing worldwide shipments of liquefied natural gas make its price more uniform. Meanwhile, other once-celebrated commodities have lost their claim to fame. With the 1958 Onion Futures Act, America banned futures trading of onions, after two men cornered the Chicago market. The frozen concentrated-orange-juice market is being squeezed despite Eddie Murphy's best efforts to popularise it in *Trading Places* – consumers are opting for fresh varieties. In 2011, the Chicago Mercantile Exchange even stopped offering trade in frozen pork-belly futures. Some commodities may have existed since before the dawn of mankind. But not all of them will be commodities for ever.

Does longevity always increase with national wealth?

"In the end, it is not the years in your life that count. It is the life in your years," goes the saying. Many people fear that a trade-off between the two is inevitable: they may live to a very old age, but their final years may be spent in wretched health. Data from 30 European countries suggest that such a trade-off depends on where people live, and whether they are men or women. The number of years of healthy life that the average person can expect can be determined from a survey asking people about long-term health problems that limit their usual daily activities. On average, European women who turn 65 can expect to live about three years longer than men at that age, who have a life expectancy of 17.4 more years. However, women tend to spend much of that extra time in poor health; the number of healthy years for men and women is the same, at just over nine.

Does it help to live in one of Europe's richer countries? The data

Live long and prosper

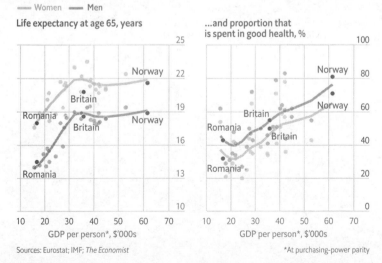

— Women — Men

Life expectancy at age 65, years

...and proportion that is spent in good health, %

Sources: Eurostat; IMF; *The Economist*

*At purchasing-power parity

suggest that life expectancy at age 65 rises with a country's wealth, but only up to a point. The trend levels off at a GDP per person of around $30,000 (adjusted for differences in price levels between countries), which is roughly the dividing line between eastern and western Europe. By contrast, the time spent in good health increases in a linear fashion with a country's wealth. Italian 65-year-olds, for example, can expect to live about the same number of years as Norwegian ones, even though Norway is much richer than Italy. But Norway's elderly are likely to spend nearly 80% of their remaining time in good health, whereas those in Italy can hope for just 40%.

This may be a result of countries' spending on public services and infrastructure. Many characteristic health problems of old age, such as difficulties with hearing or eyesight, are not fatal; but unless they are dealt with, and unless public spaces are adapted to the needs of the elderly, they can make life miserable. Pavements, street signs and pedestrian signals, for example, are often designed for the young and able-bodied. Richer countries have more money to spend on making them better suited to older age groups. That may not extend lifespans, but it can help people make the most of their remaining years.

Why do companies exist?

The idea of the price mechanism is central to the study of economics. Market prices convey information about what people want to buy and what others want to sell. Adam Smith used the metaphor of the "invisible hand" to describe how the economy is governed by price signals. In 1937 a paper published by Ronald Coase, a British economist, pointed out a flaw in this view: it did not explain what goes on within firms. When employees switch from one division to another, for instance, they do not do so in response to higher wages, but because they are ordered to. The question posed by Coase was a profound, if awkward, one for economics. Why do firms exist?

His answer was that firms are a response to the high cost of using markets. It is often cheaper to direct tasks by fiat than to negotiate and enforce separate contracts for every transaction. Such "exchange costs" are low in markets for uniform goods, wrote Coase, but are high in other instances. But his answer only raised further tricky questions. For instance, if the reason firms exist is to reduce transaction costs, why have market transactions at all?

To address such questions, economists have developed a theory of contracts, which makes a distinction between spot transactions and business dealings that require longer-term co-operation. Most transactions take place in spot markets. They are well suited to simple, low-value transactions, such as buying a newspaper or taking a taxi. And they are governed by market forces, as lots of buyers bargain over the price of similar goods. Things become trickier for goods or services that are not standardised. Parties to a transaction are then required to make commitments to each other that are costly to reverse. Take a property lease. A business that is evicted from its premises could not quickly find something similar. Equally, if a tenant suddenly quit, the landlord would be stuck. Each could threaten the other in a bid for a better rent. A long-term contract that specifies the rent, tenure and so on protects both parties from the opportunism of the other. For many business arrangements, it is difficult to set down all that is required of each party in all circumstances. This is where an "incomplete" contract has advantages. A marriage contract is of this kind. So is an employment contract. It has a few formal terms: job title, working hours, initial pay, and so on, but many of the most important duties are not written down. It cannot be enforced by the courts because its obligations are implicit. It stays in force mostly because its breakdown would hurt both parties. Because market forces are softened in such a contract, an alternative form of governance is required, which is the firm.

Coase argued that the degree to which the firm stands in for the market will vary with changing circumstances. Eighty years on, the boundary between the two might appear to be dissolving altogether. The share of self-employed contractors in the labour force has risen. The "gig economy", exemplified by Uber drivers, is mushrooming. Yet firms are not withering away, nor are they likely to. Prior to Uber, taxi-drivers in most cities were already self-employed. Spot-like job contracts are becoming more common, but their flexibility comes at a cost. Workers have little incentive to invest in firm-specific skills, so productivity suffers. The supply chains for complex goods, such as an iPhone or an Airbus A380 superjumbo, rely on long-term contracts between firms that are "incomplete". Coase was the first to spot an enduring truth: economies need both the benign dictatorship of the firm and the invisible hand of the market.

Millennial Americans are just as loyal to their employers as previous generations

It is often claimed that millennials (people born between 1982 and 1999) are fickle employees, changing jobs frequently and reluctant to commit themselves to a single employer for the long term.

Millennials are indeed more likely to switch jobs than their older colleagues. But that is more a result of how old they are than of the era they were born in: young people at the start of their working lives have always job-hopped more than older people who are more established in their careers. In America at least, average job tenures have barely changed in recent decades.

Data from America's Bureau of Labour Statistics show that workers aged 25 and over now spend a median of 5.1 years with their employers, slightly more than in 1983 (see chart). Job tenure has declined for the lower end of that age group, but only slightly. Men between the ages of 25 and 34 now spend a median of 2.9 years with each employer, down from 3.2 years in 1983.

Labour immobility

United States, median years spent at job
By sex and age

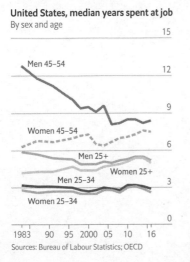

Average years spent at job
By country and age

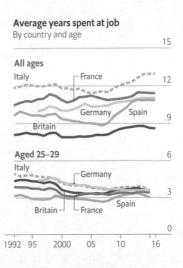

Sources: Bureau of Labour Statistics; OECD

It is middle-aged men whose relationship with their employers has changed most dramatically. Partly because of a collapse in the number of semi-skilled jobs and the decline of labour unions, the median job tenure for men aged 45–54 in America has fallen from 12.8 years in 1983 to 8.4. That decline has been offset by women staying longer in their jobs and higher retirement ages, which is why the overall numbers have barely changed.

One place where millennials probably are switching jobs more often is western Europe. Data from the OECD, a club of mostly rich countries, show that since 1992 in each of France, Germany, Italy and Spain, the average job tenure for workers has increased overall. But it has shortened for younger workers. However, it is far from clear that this is by the young workers' choice. Labour-market restrictions in Europe have forced a growing share of workers into temporary "gigs". Over half of workers aged 15 to 24 in those four countries are on fixed-term contracts.

Why old-fashioned manufacturing jobs aren't coming back

Manufacturing has a powerful hold over politicians and policymakers in the rich world. Donald Trump, among others, wants to bring the job of making things back to America from the low-cost countries to which it has emigrated. Manufacturing is worthy of political attention. Manufacturers are more likely to be exporters than other types of businesses, and exporters tend to be more productive than non-exporting firms. But when politicians talk about manufacturing it tends to be in terms of the production line: assembling parts into cars, washing machines or aircraft, which adds less value than it once did. It is the processes that accompany assembly – design, supply-chain management, servicing – that today add the most value. Manufacturing, and jobs in manufacturing, have changed in ways that mean that the old jobs will never return to the rich world.

Because of these changes, working out how many people are employed in manufacturing is tricky. Between the 1840s and the 1960s in Britain, manufacturing's share of employment hovered at around a third; today, official data show around one worker in ten is involved in manufacturing. In the late 1940s in America, it accounted for one in three non-farm jobs. Today's figure is just one in 11. But the way official figures are compiled means that manufacturing's decline has been exaggerated. Some processes that used to be tightly held together are now strung out across the world. Manufacturing companies increasingly outsource tasks such as marketing or accounting. That may mean that manufacturers employ fewer people, even if the number of people actually working on the assembly line is unchanged. As a result, the decline in manufacturing jobs looks bigger than it really is.

These trends seem set to continue. Many aspects of R&D, product design and technical testing are now looked after by separate companies, along with lots of accounting, logistics, cleaning, personnel management and IT services. A study published in 2015 by the Brookings Institution, an American think-tank, reckoned that the 11.5m American jobs counted as manufacturing employment in 2010 were outnumbered almost two to one by jobs in manufacturing-related services: added, the total would be 32.9m. In future, service providers will penetrate even deeper into manufacturers' turf, even as manufacturers come to see themselves increasingly as sellers of services. Industrial machines and the goods they turn out are increasingly packed with internet-connected sensors. Manufacturers are thus able to gather data on how their machines perform out in the world. Intimacy with the product and the data they produce helps them to turn goods into services.

This should be cheering to politicians on the lookout for manufacturing jobs. Well-paid tasks should increase in number as services related to manufacturing grow. In some fields innovation and production are increasingly interwoven. Capital-intensive high-tech manufacturing is often better done by working with the designers and engineers who thought up the products. As that suggests, though, the potential for new jobs in manufacturing is not quite the boon politicians would like. Advanced manufacturing provides good jobs but they demand skill and adaptability. Improved education to ensure that engineers and techies are in good supply is required, as is vocational training, along the lines that Germany uses to support schemes to update the skills of current and former workers. Simply threatening companies that seek to move jobs overseas, as Mr Trump has done, will not help. Using tariffs to disrupt the complex cross-border supply chains on which manufacturers rely, another of his favoured approaches, damages the sectors he purports to champion. Clamping down on migrants who have skills that manufacturers cannot find at home will do further harm. And policies that favour production-line workers over investment in automation will end up making domestic industry less competitive. That is why it is important to recognise what a manufacturing job looks like these days.

Why India scrapped its two biggest bank notes

In a surprise televised address on the evening of November 8th 2016, Narendra Modi, the prime minister of India, delivered a bombshell: most of the money in Indians' wallets would cease to be accepted in shops at midnight. The two most valuable notes, of 500 and 1,000 rupees ($7.50 and $15), were to be "demonetised" – in other words, taken out of circulation. Indians were given until the end of the year to visit banks to either exchange their cash against newly printed notes or deposit it in their accounts. After that, the old notes would become mere pieces of printed paper with no value at all. The notes being nixed represented 86% of all cash in circulation. Citizens and businesses faced weeks of disruption as the new currency was deployed. So why did the Indian government do it?

The government justified the move in part due to concerns over a proliferation of counterfeit notes (not unusually, it pointed the finger at neighbouring Pakistan), which it claimed was fuelling the drug trade and funding terrorism. But the main target was "black money", cash from undeclared sources which sits outside the financial system. Perhaps 20% of India's economy is informal. Some of that is poor farmers, who are largely exempt from tax anyway. But the rich are perceived to be sitting on a vast illicit hoard. Though a large part of that sits in bank accounts in predictable foreign jurisdictions, a chunk of it was held in high-value Indian notes. Purchases of gold or high-end real estate have long been made at least in part with bundles (or suitcases) of illicit cash.

The impact of the move was that everyone had to disclose all their cash or face losing it. Those with a few bundles of 500-rupee notes clearly weren't the target: the government said tax authorities would not be informed of deposits of less than 250,000 rupees. But its sudden announcement put those who had amassed large piles of notes in a bind. An amnesty programme for "black money" had just come to an end, so the tax man was unlikely to look upon undeclared cash piles with sympathy. As they queued up to exchange their notes, the comfort for the poor was that the greedy, tax-dodging rich would suffer more, as they struggled to launder their suitcases full of cash by year-end.

That was the theory, anyway. But a report from the central bank, the Reserve Bank of India (RBI), in August 2017 revealed that of the 15.4trn rupees ($241bn) of banknotes withdrawn, 15.3trn rupees, or 99% of them, had been accounted for. Either the "black money" never existed or, more likely, the hoarders found ways to make it legitimate. Defenders of the demonetisation scheme insisted that it was merely one plank of a wider fight against informal economic activity and corruption. Officials had once privately salivated in hope that maybe a quarter of the money, if not more, would remain in the shadows. Social-media rumours had suggested that this could finance a one-off dividend to be dished out to all Indians. But with 99% of the money accounted for, the dividend would have amounted to only 100 rupees per person. The whole episode dented the RBI's reputation for independence and competence. It also hit national pride: the demonetisation scheme constrained economic growth, thus handing back to China India's coveted crown of being the world's fastest-growing large economy.

The roots of the gender pay gap lie in childhood

It is well known that parenthood tends to hurt women's careers but not men's. Numerous studies have shown that having children lowers women's lifetime earnings, an outcome known as the "child penalty". A wide range of individual decisions account for this effect. Some women work fewer hours, or not at all, when their children are young. Others switch to jobs that are more family-friendly but lower-paid. There is substantial variation in the size of the earnings decline, ranging from zero all the way up to 100% (in the case of women who stop working altogether).

Yet there is an intriguing factor that helps to predict whether the reduction in a woman's income due to having children is likely to be large or small: the choices made during her childhood by her own mother. A study by Henrik Kleven from Princeton University, Camille Landais from the London School of Economics and Jakob Sogaard from the Danish Ministry of Taxation analysed administrative data from Denmark, which covers the country's entire population for generations, to quantify the child penalty,

Like mother, like daughter

April–May 2015

Earnings relative to pre-child earnings, %

Years before/after birth of first child

Fall in mothers' long-term earnings due to children, %

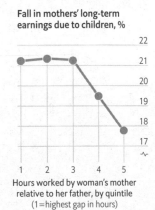

Hours worked by woman's mother relative to her father, by quintile (1=highest gap in hours)

Source: "Children and Gender Inequality: Evidence from Denmark" by H. Kleven, C. Landais and J. Søgaard

defined as the amount by which women's earnings fell behind those of men after having children. From 1980 to 2013, the long-run child penalty was found to be about 20%. Because the overall pay gap between men and women shrank during that period, by 2013 the child penalty accounted for almost the entire remaining difference in the sexes' incomes. Before becoming mothers, women's compensation more or less keeps pace with men's. Only once they have children do their economic trajectories begin to lag.

As the researchers explored potential causes for this phenomenon, they noticed that women who grew up in families in which the mother worked a lot relative to the father tended to suffer relatively smaller child penalties. Conversely, those who grew up with stay-at-home mothers were more likely to scale back their careers. This suggests that women are heavily influenced by the examples set by their own mothers when deciding how to balance work and family. Tellingly, the working patterns of a woman's parents-in-law made no difference to her child penalty, suggesting that women's decisions are not influenced by preferences that their partners may have formed during childhood. All of which is a lesson to those mothers who want their daughters to bridge the gender pay gap. Their wishes are more likely to come true if they lead by example when their girls are young.

Department of white coats: science, health and the environment

Can young blood really rejuvenate the old?

The vampire jokes write themselves. In the past few years a steady trickle of scientific papers has suggested something straight out of an airport horror novel: that the blood of young animals, infused into the old, has rejuvenating effects. Scientists are excited enough that at least two clinical trials are being undertaken in humans. But is it true? And if it is, how does it work?

The answer to the first question seems to be a qualified yes, at least in animals. The rejuvenating effects of young blood are seen when lab mice are joined together in a rather gruesome procedure called parabiosis. That involves making cuts in the skin of two animals, then suturing them together at the site of the wound. As the cuts heal, the pair's blood vessels grow together and merge. The result is two animals that share a circulatory system, with both hearts pumping both sets of blood around both bodies. Doing this with an old mouse and a young mouse has some spectacular effects. As with humans, old mice have a harder time than younger ones healing from injuries. But link an old mouse to a young one and it becomes able to repair muscle injuries nearly as well as its younger counterpart. Similar benefits are seen in liver cells and the nervous system. And it works in reverse, too: old blood can have a decrepifying effect on the young.

Exactly how this all works is much less clear. The best guess is that some combination of hormones, signalling factors and other ingredients in the young blood affects the behaviour of stem cells in the old animal. Like everything else, stem cells – which are vital for healing wounds and for general maintenance – begin to fail with age. But that process seems to be reversible, with young blood restoring the cells' ability to proliferate and mend broken tissue. Another theory is that the old animal benefits from access to the organs (kidneys, liver and so on) of its young companion. It may be that both explanations are correct: experiments in which animals are given quick transfusions, rather than being stitched together for weeks, still show benefits, though not as many as with full-on parabiosis.

That uncertainty has not stopped people jumping into trials with humans. One company, called Alkahest, has recruited 18 people with Alzheimer's disease. It plans to give them regular blood transfusions from young donors. The trial is primarily designed to prove that the treatment is safe. But because blood transfusions are already routine, Alkahest hopes that will be easy, and plans to look for mental benefits, too. Another company, Ambrosia, has raised eyebrows by charging people $8,000 to take part in its clinical trial, which will see people over 35 receiving blood from under-25s. It is far from clear whether any of this will work (anti-ageing research is dogged by cycles of hype and disappointment). And if it does, there is already a perennial shortage of donated blood, and it is needed for surgery and medical emergencies more than for speculative anti-ageing therapies. The best-case scenario is that blood compounds will indeed turn out to be responsible for the salutary effects; that scientists will be able to identify them; and that biochemists will work out a way to mass-produce them as drugs. Even then, the result would not necessarily be a life-extension potion. The hope instead is to extend "healthspan", keeping elderly people hale and hearty for longer. Not the immortality of vampires, then, but still an outcome worth pursuing.

What people want at the end of life

As death approaches, what do most people want, hope for and worry about? In 2016 *The Economist* and the Kaiser Family Foundation, an American non-profit focused on health care, polled people in America, Brazil, Italy and Japan to find out. What is most important to people depends on where they live. In America and Japan not burdening families with the cost of care was the highest-ranked priority. (The Japanese may be worrying about the cost of funerals, which can easily reach ¥3m, or $24,000; Americans may be worrying about medical bills, which can be ruinous.) In Brazil, where Catholicism prevails, the leading priority was being at peace spiritually. What Italians wanted most at the end was to have their loved ones around them. Doctors' efforts to extend life near its end may not always be aligned with their patients' priorities: living as long as possible was deemed least important of seven options, except in Brazil where it tied with not burdening relatives financially.

The majority of people in each country had given "some" or "a great deal" of thought to their wishes for medical treatment in case of serious illness. But having spoken with their families

Last orders

Thinking about your own death, how important is:
2016, % replying "extremely" or "very important"

United States Italy Japan Brazil

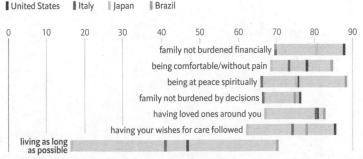

Source: Kaiser Family Foundation/*The Economist*

about the subject was much less common, and putting wishes down in writing even rarer. Americans were most likely to have planned ahead: 56% had spoken with a loved one about the medical treatment they wanted if the event of serious illness; 27% had put their wishes in a written document. The Japanese were the most likely to have avoided the subject, even though Japan has the world's oldest population. Less than a third had told their families about their wishes in case of serious illness and only 6% had put those wishes in writing.

In all four countries polled, there was a big discrepancy between what people wanted and what they expected to happen to them at the end. Majorities in each said that if they could choose where to die, they would die at home. Americans felt that particularly strongly, with nearly two-thirds preferring to die at home. In each of the four countries, however, the share who thought they were most likely to die at home fell about 30 percentage points short of the share who hoped to. Expecting to die in hospital was far more common than wishing to die there.

Around the world, the taboo on talking about death is starting to fade. Over time, that should help narrow the gap between what people want for their deaths, and what they are likely to get. Though death is inevitable, a bad death is not.

How China reduced its air pollution

"I've never seen Beijing like this," said Emmanuel Macron, the French president, beneath a cloudless blue sky at the end of a visit in January 2018. The next day Greenpeace East Asia, an NGO, showed that his impression was accurate. It found that concentrations of PM2.5 – the smallest polluting particles, which pose the greatest health risks – were 54% lower in the Chinese capital during the fourth quarter of 2017 than during the same period in 2016. Concentrations of PM2.5 in 26 cities across northern China, clustered around Beijing and Tianjin, were one-third lower. China genuinely has reduced its notorious air pollution. How has it done it, and at what cost?

The country has had draconian anti-pollution measures in place since 2013, when it introduced a set of prohibitions called the national action plan on air pollution. This imposed a nationwide cap on coal use, divided up among provinces, so that Beijing (for instance) had to reduce its coal consumption by 50% between 2013 and 2018. The plan banned new coal-burning capacity (though power stations already in the works were allowed) and sped up the installation of filters and scrubbers. All this cut levels of PM2.5 in Beijing by more than a quarter between 2013, the time of the city's notorious "airpocalypse", and 2016. The measures were notable for being outright bans on polluting activities, rather than incentives to clean up production, such as prices or taxes (though China has those, too, including what is expected to become the world's largest carbon market).

The improvement in air quality in northern China was also helped by further command-and-control measures, which were imposed in October 2017. Air pollution spikes in northern China during the winter, because most domestic heating is fuelled by coal. The 26 northern cities, again with Beijing and Tianjin, imposed output controls on steel and aluminium smelters. They mothballed large construction projects in order to reduce smog from cement production and diesel trucks. And they created a new environmental protection agency, with tough enforcement powers, in Beijing and its surroundings. These prohibitions were so tough that in some areas they forced the authorities into an unusual U-turn. The cities had promised to convert almost 4m households from coal-burning to electricity or gas in 2017, and they shut off the use of coal in houses, hospitals and schools even before the replacement systems were ready. When hospital wards froze and schools took to holding classes in sub-zero playgrounds (where at least it was sunny), the government had to allow some coal-burning after all.

The drop in pollution in late 2017 illustrates why bans in China often work better than elsewhere. First, many of the biggest polluters are state-owned, and so are more easily controlled. Second, with more than half of China's pollution coming from coal-fired power stations, the government can concentrate on reducing the use of coal, unlike governments in places where the causes of pollution are more varied. Even so, command-and-control measures were most effective when the composition of GDP was anyway switching from heavy industry and infrastructure towards services, as it was from 2013 to 2016. When infrastructure spending rose again, as it did in 2016 and 2017, such measures were unable to do more than stop emissions rising, too. Prohibitions in northern China also seem to have shifted some polluting activities elsewhere. National levels of PM2.5 were only 4.5% lower in 2017 than in 2016, which implies that pollution increased in southern China. Moreover, the costs are high, even leaving aside the impact on schools and hospitals. In 2015 the Clean Air Alliance of China, an advisory group, reckoned that the investment cost of the 2013–18 national plan in Beijing, Tianjin and the surrounding province of Hebei would be 250bn yuan ($38bn). That does not include the opportunity cost of suspending whole industries and construction projects for months on end. In short, China's measures work, but at a price. The country has won battles against air pollution, but not yet the war.

Why forests are spreading in the rich world

Forests in countries like Brazil and Congo get a lot of attention from conservationists, and it is easy to see why. South America and sub-Saharan Africa are experiencing deforestation on an enormous scale: every year almost 5m hectares are lost. But forests are also changing in rich Western countries. They are growing larger, in two senses: they occupy more land, and the trees in them are bigger. What is going on?

Forests are spreading in almost all Western countries, with the fastest growth in places that historically had rather few trees. In 1990 28% of Spain was forested; now the proportion is 37%. In both Greece and Italy, the growth was from 26% to 32% over the same period. Forests are gradually taking more land in America and Australia. Perhaps most astonishing is the trend in Ireland. Roughly 1% of that country was forested when it became independent in 1922. Now forests cover 11% of the land, and the government wants to push the proportion up to 18% by the 2040s.

Two things are fertilising this growth. The first is the abandonment of farmland, especially in high, parched places where nothing grows terribly well. When farmers give up trying to eke out a living from olives or sheep, trees simply move in. The second is government policy and subsidies. Governments have protected and promoted forests over the centuries for many reasons, ranging from the need to build wooden warships to a desire to promote suburban house-building. These days they increasingly welcome forests because they are carbon sinks. The justifications change; the desire for more trees remains constant.

The greening of the West does not delight everyone. Farmers complain that land is being taken out of use by generously subsidised tree plantations. (Farmers get subsidies too, but the ones for tree-planting are especially generous.) Parts of Spain and Portugal are afflicted by terrible forest fires. These burn especially hot in areas with lots of eucalyptus trees – an Australian import that was planted for its pulp but has spread of its own accord. Some people simply dislike the appearance of conifer forests planted in neat rows. They will have to get used to the trees, however. The growth of Western forests seems almost as inexorable as the deforestation taking place elsewhere.

The Arctic could be ice-free by 2040, 30 years sooner than expected

Over the past three decades the area of sea ice in the Arctic has fallen by more than half and its volume has plummeted by three-quarters. So says a report "Snow, Water, Ice, Permafrost in the Arctic" (SWIPA), produced under the auspices of the Arctic Council, a scientific-policy club for the eight countries with territory in the Arctic Circle, as well as observers including China and India. SWIPA estimates that the Arctic will be free of sea ice in the summer by 2040. Scientists previously suggested this would not occur until 2070. The thickness of ice in the central Arctic ocean declined by

Arctic sea ice extent

Source: National Snow and Ice Data Centre

*Area of ocean with at least 15% sea ice

65% between 1975 and 2012; record lows in the maximum extent of Arctic sea ice occurred in March 2017.

In theory, shipping firms should benefit from access to a more open seaway. Using the Arctic to sail from northern Europe to northeast Asia can cut the length of voyages by two-fifths compared with travelling via the Suez Canal. But any Arctic promise has drifted away and the expected shipping boom has not materialised. In 2012 only 1m tonnes of goods were shipped through the northern passage, a paltry level of activity and one not achieved since. That is because even in the summer months the Arctic ocean is stormy, making timely delivery of goods impossible to guarantee. Drifting ice also poses a danger. Ships must be strengthened to withstand it, adding to construction costs. And a lack of coastal infrastructure, such as deepwater ports, means that spills of the heavy fuel-oil that powers most vessels could wreak havoc on both ecosystems and reputations, because clean-up missions would have to set out from much farther away and would take much longer to be effective.

A new polar code from the International Maritime Organisation, which regulates shipping, came into force at the beginning of 2017 to try to address some of these concerns. It bans discharges of sewage and oily mixtures in polar waters. America and Canada, among others, want to go further. For one thing, they want a ban on heavy fuel-oil (as there is in the Antarctic, which has various special protections).

Nothing, however, looms larger than the potential for environmental calamity. The question of Arctic thawing is moving up the list of priorities both of countries with territory in the region and those farther afield. An unusual heatwave in the Arctic in February 2018, combined with particularly cold weather in Europe, raised concerns that warming could be undermining the northern polar vortex, a persistent low-pressure zone that keeps cold air trapped around the pole. Sticking to the Paris agreement could, eventually, stabilise temperatures. But more radical measures may be needed, given that countries are unlikely to keep within the limits set in Paris.

Why there's something in the water in New Zealand

Windy cattle have always had an impact on their environment. But in New Zealand, where pastures that once grazed sheep have been converted into dairy farms to feed China's appetite for milk, the situation is particularly noxious. Bovine burps (for these are the main problem) have contributed to a 23% rise in New Zealand's greenhouse-gas emissions since 1990. Agriculture accounts for almost half of total emissions, a far higher share than in other rich countries. Consultants reckon that New Zealand needs to cut livestock numbers to meet its target of reducing greenhouse-gas emissions by 30% below 2005 levels by 2030. But gas is not the only problematic excretion. A second, less familiar environmental worry has emerged in a country that stakes its reputation on its purity. The bodily waste of the 6.6m dairy cattle has sullied rivers and groundwater. Almost two-thirds of the country's waterways are now unsafe for swimming.

Cows pollute water in a couple of ways. Their nitrogen-rich urine leaches off soil into waterways, where it acts like a fertiliser. Together with phosphorus, which is carried into rivers in soil particles, it can cause slime and toxic algae to grow. Half of monitored river sites in New Zealand contain enough nitrogen to trigger algal blooms, according to the OECD, a club of mostly rich countries. Toxic algae has killed at least 70 dogs since 2006. Across the intensively farmed Canterbury plains, pregnant women are advised to test drinking water for nitrates to avoid blue-baby syndrome, an ailment which can suffocate infants. But it is ecosystems that are most at risk. Too much nitrogen is toxic to fish, and excessive growth of algae depletes the oxygen in the water. Ecologists blame these pollutants for putting almost three-quarters of native fish under threat.

Further damage comes from manure, which carries nasty bacteria such as *E. coli*. Cows have an unfortunate fondness for wading, which means that their faeces are often deposited in water. New Zealanders are twice as likely as Britons to fall sick from campylobacter, another bug harboured in cow dung, and are three times more vulnerable than Australians. Doctors say there is a relatively high incidence of gastroenteritis in Canterbury, a region of New Zealand's South Island with lots of cows and untreated water.

All this frustrates New Zealanders. Some worry about the impact on tourism, the only export industry that is more important than dairy farming. Over 3m people visit New Zealand annually, expecting it to be, as the tourism campaign promises, "100% Pure". They might turn away if pollution worsens. Farmers have responded by fencing off rivers to prevent cows from wading in, and planting trees to curb soil erosion. Regional councils are required, at least in theory, to set limits for water quality to ensure that it does not diminish further. In 2017 a plan was hatched to make 90% of rivers safe for swimming by 2040. Yet many environmentalists were disappointed by the high level of the government-imposed guidelines for nitrates in water, which made rivers look safer than many believe them to be. As with emissions, ecologists argue that it is impossible to clean up water without first cutting the national herd. Even the government's agriculture minister admits that the nation may have got close to the "maximum number of cows".

Measures to discourage smoking are spreading around the world

Every two years the World Health Organisation (WHO) takes stock of the efforts of governments around the globe to curb smoking. Its latest report, published in July 2017, shows that only a single country, Turkey, has implemented to the fullest degree all of the measures recommended by the WHO. These include smoking bans,

Can you kick it?

Number of countries introducing strict* tobacco-control policies, 1999–2016, cumulative

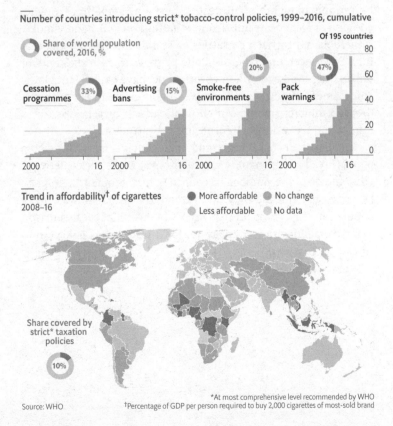

Source: WHO

*At most comprehensive level recommended by WHO
†Percentage of GDP per person required to buy 2,000 cigarettes of most-sold brand

high cigarette taxes, warnings about the dangers of smoking, bans on tobacco advertising and publicly subsidised services that help smokers quit.

Although the number of countries adopting such measures has steadily grown, loopholes remain common. Outside Europe, taxes on cigarettes tend to be low. As a result, smoking in the rest of the world was just as affordable in 2016 as it was in 2008 – and in many places it has become cheaper. Only a tenth of the world's population lives in countries where taxes make up at least three-quarters of the price of cigarettes, the level that has been shown to be effective in discouraging smoking.

Around an eighth of all deaths caused by smoking – roughly 900,000 a year – result from inhaling second-hand smoke. Nonetheless, nearly 60 countries have no bans on smoking that fully cover even one type of public place, such as restaurants or universities. And even when governments have passed strict laws, enforcement often ranges from lax to non-existent. For example, Greece prohibits smoking in all public places, yet any visitor to Athens will see residents lighting up with abandon.

The most encouraging trend in recent years is the rising popularity of strong graphic warnings on cigarette packs. Between 2014 and 2016 the number of countries that adopted them grew by three-quarters, and they now extend to nearly half the world's population. This sharp jump gives public-health advocates reason to hope that other proven measures to curb smoking could start to spread faster as well.

Why "gene drives" have yet to be deployed in the wild

The chance that a sexually reproducing organism's offspring will inherit a particular version of a gene from a particular parent is usually 50%. "Gene drives" are stretches of DNA that change those odds to favour one parent's version of a gene over the other's. If the odds are stacked sufficiently in favour of one version, then within a few generations it can become the only version of the gene still in circulation within a given population. This could be a useful property. Soon after the discovery of gene drives in nature, half a century ago, researchers realised that they could be made into powerful tools for eradicating diseases and pests. A gene drive spreading a gene that makes mosquitoes unable to host the parasite that causes malaria could eliminate the disease, for example. If the drive makes female mosquitoes sterile, it could eliminate the insect altogether. Yet no such gene drive has been released into the wild. Why not?

Early attempts to produce a synthetic gene drive focused on enzymes called homing endonucleases. These can insert copies of the genes that encode them into chromosomes, thus increasing both their number and the likelihood that they will be passed on to the organism's progeny. Engineering these to do humanity's bidding (by disrupting fertility genes, for example) proved difficult. That problem was solved in 2015, though, when Valentino Gantz and Ethan Bier of the University of California, San Diego, used CRISPR-Cas9, a recently discovered gene-editing tool, to make a gene drive that could be inserted anywhere in the genome of a fruit fly.

The ease with which gene drives can be made with CRISPR-Cas9 has, however, provoked fresh worries about the technique, which would have to be addressed before gene-drive-carrying organisms could be let loose in the wild. First, a gene drive that somehow hopped from a target species into the genomes of other animals might wipe them out before anything could be done about it. Researchers are therefore developing ways to switch off gene drives. Second, some ecologists worry about the side-effects of exterminating entire species. Kill off malaria-carrying mosquitoes, for example, and animals that feed on them and their larvae will also suffer. Third, it is doubtful that all countries would agree to organisms harbouring gene drives being deployed on their soil. So there would need to be some means of confining the drive's effects to a particular area. Initial trials of the technology are likely to be run on small, uninhabited islands. Finally, a study published in 2017 in the journal *PLOS Genetics* added to the evidence that gene drives simply may not work. Just as insects and pathogens evolve resistance to new pesticides and antibiotics, so gene drives, too, may provoke resistance. They may do so far faster than many suspect.

None of this means that gene drives will not eventually fulfil their promise. Researchers continue to work on drives intended to eliminate malaria and mosquitoes, and to create mice that cannot bear daughters, to wipe out invasive rodents. Others are trying to create white-footed mice that would be immune to infection by the bacteria that cause Lyme disease. That would prevent the ticks that eventually transmit the disease to people from becoming infected when they feed on the mice. Gene drives are also expected to play a role in the government of New Zealand's plan to rid that country of all rats, stoats and possums by 2050. Nonetheless, the study in *PLOS Genetics* strengthens the case that tricking evolution will be hard. To paraphrase *Jurassic Park*, life finds a way.

Why it is so hard to fix India's sanitation problems

India vies with China to be the world's fastest-growing large economy, but its record on basic sanitation is dreadful. Around 450m people relieve themselves in playgrounds, behind trees, by roadsides, and on railway tracks and river banks. In cities, 157m urban dwellers, more than the population of Russia, lack decent toilet facilities. Much of the solid waste is emptied into rivers, lakes and ponds untreated. The World Bank says one in ten deaths in India is linked to poor sanitation. From contaminated groundwater, children pick up chronic infections that impair their bodies' ability to absorb nutrients. Almost 44m children under five, says the bank, have stunted growth, and every year more than 300,000 die from diarrheal diseases. What can India do to change this grim reality?

In 2014 the government pledged to end open defecation by 2019. That year marks the 150th anniversary of the birth of Mahatma Gandhi, who considered sanitation to be sacred and "more important than political freedom". Authorities have set aside $29bn for the nationwide programme, which claims to have constructed 49m household toilets to date, with another 61m still to go. Families get 12,000 rupees ($187) to build a toilet. The initiative is part of a long line of schemes that go back to the country's first five-year plan of the early 1950s. The Indian government has been subsidising lavatories in remote villages for over three decades. Between 1986 and 1999 it installed 9.4m latrines, giving 7.4m more people access to sanitation every year. But improved coverage does not guarantee greater usage. A survey by the Research Institute for Compassionate Economics in 2014 found that in 40% of households with a working toilet, at least one family member preferred to defecate outside.

People in villages often fail to acknowledge that a lack of sanitation is a problem. Many use toilets only in emergencies, worrying that the cesspits will clog up quickly when, in fact, they are meant to last a family of five about ten years. Caste division plays a part, too. Villagers are reluctant to empty latrine pits manually, a task relegated historically to *dalits* (formerly untouchables). Some consider defecating in the open to be a sign of virility, and believe a stroll to the fields aids digestion. Toilets, often the only concrete structure in a house, may end up being used to store firewood, grass, chickens, cow-dung cakes and food grains, or double up as goat-sheds. Implementation of the scheme is patchy, too. Families who receive a toilet-building subsidy do not always build one. Often the *sarpanch* (village head), the junior engineer who surveys the site and the local contractor are in cahoots and skimp on building materials and design, says Nitya Jacob, a sanitation consultant.

Simply punching holes in the ground at breakneck speed will not solve the problem. India could learn from neighbouring Bangladesh, which reduced the prevalence of open defecation from 34% to 1% between 1990 and 2015. As part of a sustained effort, its government partnered with village councils to educate people in the merits of good sanitation. Instead of just highlighting the hazards of open defecation, it extolled the virtues of clean sanitation. Having a toilet became a symbol of dignity. Women decided on the location and type of toilets to be built in their homes. In India, by contrast, officials have at times brutally punished those who defecate outside, either by having them beaten up, or denying them government benefits like pensions and monthly household provisions unless they build a toilet at home. In the short term such coercive tactics might work to increase the number of installed toilets. But they will do little to promote their use.

Why some deadly diseases are hard to eradicate

Bubonic plague brought terror to medieval Europe. Over a third of its population perished from the "Black Death" in the 14th century, hastening the end of the feudal system. As a bacterial disease, the plague these days is generally treatable with modern antibiotics. Nonetheless, it persists beyond the grim annals of history. In June 2017 health authorities in New Mexico, in the south-western United States, announced that three people had been diagnosed with

The plague

Human plague, number of reported: cases deaths
2010–15

■ Areas with potential natural focuses for plague, March 2016

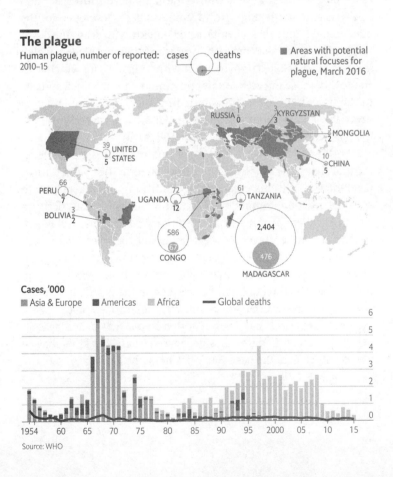

Cases, '000
■ Asia & Europe ■ Americas ■ Africa — Global deaths

Source: WHO

the disease in the previous month alone. This is a marked uptick for a country that records around seven cases a year nationwide, according to the US Centres for Disease Control and Prevention.

Zoonotic diseases such as the plague, Ebola and avian flu – which are generally carried by animals – are extremely hard to eradicate. The plague is caused by a bacterium, *Yersinia pestis*, which infects fleas, which in turn live mainly on rodents. In Europe, those fleas lived mostly on black rats. In America's south-west, the site of most cases observed in the rich world, the fleas have shifted to rural squirrels and prairie dogs. No vaccine has been developed for the plague, and if the illness is not treated quickly with drugs the death rate is high. The most common form is the bubonic plague, which is spread by flea bites or by contact with animals, and which kills 30–60% of those infected. A rarer pneumonic form, which spreads to the lungs and can be transmitted by sneezing or coughing, is invariably fatal without treatment. In America four people died of the plague in 2015, its highest annual toll for 30 years.

Worldwide, however, the plague is mainly a disease of poverty. Natural focuses – areas in which the bacteria, fleas and animal reservoirs might create the right conditions for the plague to spread – are found in much of the world. But most cases occur in countries where people live in unsanitary conditions, and where treatment may be slower. Between 2010 and 2015 there were 3,248 cases and 584 deaths. The worst-affected country is Madagascar: three-quarters of all new infections and deaths occur there. And the disease is springing up in new places on the island. In January 2017 the World Health Organisation (WHO) confirmed that 62 cases, including 26 deaths, had been reported in districts of Madagascar that had not seen an outbreak since 1950. The ancient killer may be less deadly than in the past. But it has not gone away.

Why China is sick of foreign waste

China is the world's biggest consumer of raw materials. Each year it buys billions of tonnes of crude oil, coal and iron ore. But there is one commodity market in which the country may soon play a less dominant role: waste. In July 2017 China told the World Trade Organisation that by the end of the year it would no longer accept imports of 24 categories of solid waste, as part of a government campaign against "foreign garbage". Government officials said restricting such imports would protect the environment and improve public health. But the ban affected billions of dollars in trade and put many Chinese recyclers out of business. Why was Beijing so eager to trash its trade in rubbish?

For decades China had been a major processing centre for the world's recycled waste. In 2016 the country imported 45m tonnes of scrap metal, waste paper and plastic, together worth over $18bn. Paying foreign firms for trash may have seemed like an unfair deal, but the trade benefited both sides. Exporters earned a return on their leftover waste, much of which might otherwise have ended up in a landfill. Chinese firms, meanwhile, gained access to a steady supply of recycled materials, which were often cheaper and less energy-intensive than domestically sourced raw materials – recycled steel, for example, requires 60% less energy than steel produced from iron ore.

Such economic benefits came with costs, however. Imports of recyclable waste were often dirty, poorly sorted or contaminated with hazardous substances. Even when such waste was safely imported, it was not always recycled properly. In 2002 Chinese authorities faced widespread criticism after a documentary showed workers in Guangdong province crudely dismantling discarded electronic devices and dumping the toxic remains into a river. A more recent film, *Plastic China*, examined the environmental damage caused by the country's plastic-recycling industry, which is dominated by thousands of small-scale outfits that often lack proper pollution controls. Facing growing public pressure, Chinese authorities began cracking down. In 2013 the government launched "Operation Green Fence", a campaign to block imports of illegal and low-quality waste through improved inspections of container ships. In February 2017 Chinese customs officials announced "National Sword", an initiative aimed at reducing illegal shipments of industrial and electronic waste. The ban on foreign garbage is another example of such efforts to clean up the industry.

The government says the ban will protect the environment. But analysts point out that most of the waste consumed by China's recycling industry comes from domestic sources, not imports. Waste has piled up in Western countries as exporters looked for alternative buyers in Malaysia, Vietnam or Indonesia. What cannot be sold will probably end up in a landfill.

Why are wolves coming back in France?

Residents of Lozère, a hilly department in southern France, recite complaints that can be heard in many rural corners of Europe. In remote hamlets and villages, with names such as Le Bacon and Le Bacon Vieux, mayors grumble about a lack of local schools, jobs, or phone and internet connections. Farmers of grazing animals add another, less familiar concern: the return of wolves. Eradicated from France in the 20th century, the predators are gradually creeping back to more forests and hillsides. "The wolf must be taken in hand," said an aspiring parliamentarian, Francis Palombi, when pressed by voters in an election campaign in 2017. Tourists enjoy visiting a wolf park in Lozère, but farmers fret over their livestock and their livelihoods. An official estimate suggests that France was home to some 360 wolves in 2017, up from roughly 300 in 2016. The number of packs increased from 35 to 42. Wolves have been spotted in dozens of departments in France in recent years; there was even a report of a wolf pack encircling a lone walker. Why are they back?

As early as the 9th century AD, the royal office of the Luparii – wolf-catchers – was created in France to tackle the predators. Those official hunters (and others) completed their job in the 1930s, when the last wolf disappeared from the mainland. Active hunting and improved technology such as rifles in the 19th century, plus the use of poisons, caused the population to collapse. But in the early 1990s the animals reappeared. They crossed the Alps from Italy, upsetting sheep farmers on the French side of the border. Wolves have since spread to areas such as Lozère, delighting environmentalists, who see the predators' presence as a sign of wider ecological health. Farmers, who say the wolves cause the deaths of thousands of sheep and other grazing animals, are less cheerful. They grumble that green activists and politically correct urban types have allowed the return of an old enemy.

Several factors explain the changes of the past few decades. Rural depopulation is part of the story. In Lozère, for example, farming and mining supported a population of over 140,000 residents in the mid-19th century. Today the department has fewer than 80,000 people, many in its towns. As humans withdraw, forests are expanding. In France, between 1990 and 2015, forest cover increased by an average of 102,000 hectares each year, as more fields were given over to trees. Now nearly one-third of mainland France is covered by woodland of some sort. As habitats for wolves have grown, the number of hunters has fallen. In the mid-to-late 20th century over 2m hunters regularly spent winter weekends tramping in woodland, seeking boars, birds and other prey. Today the Fédération Nationale des Chasseurs, the national hunting body, says only 1.1m people hold hunting licences, though the number of active hunters is probably lower. The protected status of wolves in Europe – hunting them is now forbidden, other than when occasional culls are sanctioned by the state – plus the efforts of NGOs to track and count the animals, have also contributed to the recovery of wolf populations.

As the lupine population of Europe spreads westwards, with occasional reports of wolves seen closer to urban areas, expect to hear of more clashes between farmers and those who celebrate the predators' return. Farmers' losses are real, but are not the only economic story. Tourist attractions, such as parks where wolves are kept and the animals' spread is discussed, also generate income and jobs in rural areas. The future of more isolated departments, such as Lozère, probably depends as much on luring tourists as on the success of farmers. The wolf can be an ally, not only a threat.

Why biggest isn't fastest in the animal kingdom

For 30 years viewers of the Discovery Channel have eagerly tuned in to *Shark Week*, an annual block of programming intended to promote understanding and conservation of the razor-toothed denizens of the deep. Although regular audiences have learned plenty about how sharks live in the wild, it had never been demonstrated that sharks can actually swim faster than humans. But in July 2017, to kick off that year's Shark Week, the channel staged the first-ever race between mankind's speediest swimmer and a great white shark. Although Michael Phelps has won 23 Olympic gold medals, the shark proved to be a tough opponent: it beat his time over 100 metres (328 feet) in open water by two full seconds, 36.1 to 38.1. In humanity's defence, the race was not held under usual conditions: for safety reasons, and to ensure the competitors did not distract

Man v beast

Body mass and maximum speed of species, by movement type

● Flying ● Running ● Swimming

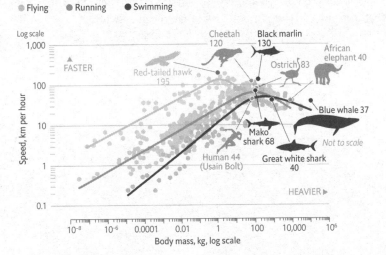

Source: "A general scaling law reveals why the largest animals are not the fastest", by Myriam Hirt et al, *Nature Ecology & Evolution*, July 2017

one another, they raced separately rather than being in the water at the same time.

Mr Phelps was merely the latest in a long line of human athletes to have fallen short in physical contests against other species. Most previous competitions involved land-dwelling adversaries, however. In 2007 a South African rugby star sprinted against a cheetah to raise awareness about the decline of the big cat. Two years later an American football player took on an ostrich, the fastest two-legged animal in the world. Both men were soundly beaten. It is unlikely that a human athlete will ever win such a race, given the species' fastest speeds.

If promoters at Discovery think that a closer contest might help lure even more viewers, they might consult a study published in *Nature Ecology & Evolution*. It examines the relationship between animals' size and their maximum velocity. The authors found that the top speed of an animal (or fish) rises in tandem with body mass up to a certain point, after which it declines. Medium-sized animals – such as cheetahs, marlins or hawks – are best for hitting a sweet spot between brawn and energy burst. The smaller Mako shark, it turns out, can swim much faster than the great white.

Geek speak: getting technical

What is a brain-computer interface?

The first computers were large machines that filled entire rooms. As they became cheaper and smaller, they moved out of basements and laboratories and closer to human beings: first to desks and laps, and eventually into pockets and on wrists. So far they have stopped – mostly – at the surface of the human body. But some computers are starting to enter the brain cavity. How would so-called "brain computers" work?

"Brain computer" is a catch-all term for a range of technologies. Definitions diverge depending on where the computer is located, and its level of processing power. Today's brain computers are relatively simple devices that exist for medical purposes and rely on crude connections to the brain. They are almost always low-power devices worn on the outside of the body, which deliver blunt signals through the skin to relevant regions of the brain. Hundreds of thousands of people already use these machines to bypass conventional input/output systems – such as fingers and voice or eyes and ears – in favour of direct communication with the brain. They are mostly used to make up for a damaged bodily function, such as hearing loss.

The simplest type of brain computer is a cochlear implant. These devices transform sound waves into electrical signals, to stimulate the auditory nerve directly. The computer controlling this process sits behind the ear, connected to a microphone and a wearable battery pack. It transmits both power and soundwaves – transformed into electromagnetic signals – to an implant just inside the skull, next to the ear. That implant receives the signal wirelessly, translates it into an electrical current and passes it down a wire, past the biological machinery of the ear, to an electrode embedded in the auditory nerve. Another sort of brain computer is called a neurostimulator, a device used in the treatment of Parkinson's disease. It is usually implanted under the skin on the chest or lower back. It sends electrical signals to parts of the brain called the basal ganglia, which are associated with control of voluntary movement.

Now a new kind of brain computer is emerging from Silicon Valley – albeit one that is, for now, still on the drawing board. Entrepreneurs think that devices could go beyond simply replacing lost functions: they dream of connecting the brain directly to computers and to the internet to give it entirely new functions that are beyond human beings' abilities today. Imagine Google searches that deliver their result to the brain before the question is consciously asked; or direct, brain-to-brain communication, in which messages are sent using thought alone. Elon Musk, with his new company Neuralink, and Bryan Johnson, with a slightly older company called Kernel, are leading the charge. For the time being, the function of the brain is not understood in enough detail to read and write information at this level of linguistic communication. But for the optimists of Silicon Valley, avid readers of science-fiction novels in which such devices are commonplace, it is only a matter of time.

The link between video games and unemployment

In 2017 the video-gaming industry racked up sales of about $110bn, making it one of the world's largest entertainment industries. The games on offer run the gamut from time-wasting smartphone apps to detailed, immersive fantasy worlds in which players can get lost for days or weeks. Indeed, the engrossing nature of games may be cause for concern. In 2016 four economists published a paper suggesting that high-quality video games – an example of what they call "leisure luxuries" – are contributing to a decline in work among young people in America, and especially young men. Given the social and economic importance of early adulthood, such a trend could spell big trouble. But are video games really causing the young to turn on and drop out?

In making the link between gaming and work, the economists Mark Aguiar, Mark Bils, Kerwin Charles and Erik Hurst point to compelling data. Between 2000 and 2015, the employment rate for men in their 20s without a college education dropped by ten percentage points, from 82% to 72%. Such men often live at their parents' homes and tend not to marry at the same rate as their peers. They, do, however, play video games. For each hour less the group spent in work, time spent at leisure activities rose by about an hour, and 75% of the increased leisure time was accounted for by gaming. Over the same period games became far more graphically and narratively complex, more social and, relative to other luxury items, more affordable. It would not be surprising if the satisfaction provided by such games kept some people from pursuing careers as aggressively as they otherwise might (or at all).

To draw a firm conclusion, however, would take a clearer understanding of the direction of causation. While games have improved since the turn of the century, labour-market options for young people have got worse. Hourly wages, adjusted for inflation, have stagnated for young college graduates since the 1990s, while pay for new high-school graduates has declined. The share of young high-school and college graduates not in work or education has risen; in 2014 about 11% of college graduates were apparently idle, compared with 9% in 2004 and 8% in 1994. The share of recent college graduates working in jobs which did not require a college degree rose from just over 30% in the early 2000s to nearly 45% a decade later. And the financial crisis and recession fell harder on young people than on the population as a whole. For people unable to find demanding, full-time work (or any work at all) gaming is often a way to spend some of one's unwanted downtime, rather than a disincentive to work; it is much more a symptom of other economic ills than a cause.

Games will go on getting better, and the share of jobless or underemployed young Americans choosing to game rather than focus on their careers will probably grow. That is not necessarily something to lament. Games are often rewarding and social, and spending time gaming indoors may provide an alternative to getting involved in undesirable or antisocial activities. If the pull of work is not strong enough to overcome the desire to game, the first response should be to ask whether more can be done to prepare young people for good jobs – and to make sure that there are some around when those young people enter the workforce.

What do robots do all day?

You have probably never heard of FANUC, the world's largest maker of industrial robots. But the chances are that you own a product built by one of its 400,000 machines. Established in 1956, the Japanese company supplies robots that build cars for Ford and Tesla, and metal iPhone cases for Apple. The firm distinguishes itself from competitors by the colour of its robots' whizzing mechanical arms, which are painted bright yellow. Its factories, offices and employee uniforms all share the same hue. FANUC is at the forefront of a booming market for robots that shows little sign of slowing. According to the International Federation of Robotics, unit sales of industrial robots grew by 15% in 2015, while revenues increased 9% to $11bn. In 2016 turnover in North America rose by 14%, to $1.8bn. ABI Research, a consultancy, reckons that the industry's sales will triple by 2025.

The popular narrative about robots is that they are stealing human workers' jobs. A paper published by the National Bureau of

The life robotic
Global industrial robots

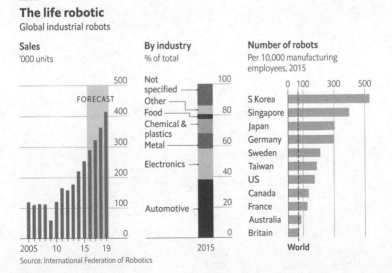

Source: International Federation of Robotics

Economic Research broadly supports this belief, estimating that each additional robot in the American economy reduces employment by 5.6 workers. But the relationship between automation and employment is not always straightforward. One big trend is the growth of "collaborative robots", smaller and more adaptable machines designed to work alongside humans and increase their productivity. Barclays, a bank, thinks that between 2016 and 2020, sales of these machines will increase more than tenfold. Adopting robots has made it economical for some manufacturers in high-wage countries to "re-shore" production from poorer countries. In 2017 Adidas, a sportswear firm, began producing running shoes in a German factory staffed by robots and 160 new workers.

FANUC is not taking its dominance for granted. The company is working on smarter, more customisable robots and is investing heavily in artificial intelligence. Its efforts to adapt in the rapidly evolving robotics industry can be seen even in the firm's new approach to colours. When the company unveiled its first collaborative robot, CR-35iA, its trademark yellow had been replaced with green.

Why 5G might be both faster and slower than previous wireless technologies

"Faster, higher, stronger," goes the Olympic motto. So it was only appropriate that the fifth generation of wireless technology, "5G" for short, should get its first showcase at the 2018 Winter Olympics in Pyeongchang, South Korea. Once fully developed, 5G is supposed to offer download speeds of at least 20 gigabits per second (4G manages about half that at best) and response times ("latency") of below 1 millisecond. That means 5G networks will be able to transfer a high-definition movie in two seconds and respond to requests in less than a hundredth of the time it takes to blink an eye. But 5G is not just about faster and broader wireless connections.

The technology could also enable all sorts of new services. One example would be real-time virtual- or augmented-reality streaming. At the Olympics, for example, many contestants were followed by 360-degree video cameras. At special venues sports fans could don virtual-reality goggles to put themselves right into the action. 5G is also supposed to become the connective tissue for the internet of things, interconnecting everything from smartphones and wireless sensors to industrial robots and self-driving cars. This will be made possible by a technique called "network slicing", which allows operators to create bespoke networks that give each set of devices exactly the kind of connectivity they need to job a particular job.

Despite its versatility, it is not clear how quickly 5G will take off. The biggest brake will be economic. When the GSMA, an industry group, asked 750 telecoms bosses in 2017 about the most salient impediment to delivering 5G, more than half cited the lack of a clear business case. People may always want more bandwidth, but they are not willing to pay much more for it – an attitude that even the lure of the fanciest virtual-reality applications may not change. And building 5G networks will not be cheap. Because they operate at higher radio frequencies, 5G networks will require more antennae, base stations and fibre-optic cables.

Although it can deliver data more quickly, 5G technology will arrive slowly. Analysts expect network operators to roll out 5G more gradually than the previous wireless generation – and only in places where the numbers add up. Some will initially use the technology to provide super-fast "fixed" wireless links between stationary antennae, which is less tricky to do. Others may use 5G to get more out of the spectrum they already own. Yet others will focus on building 5G networks to serve densely populated cities. In other words, 5G's trajectory is likely to resemble that of 3G, which was launched in the early 2000s. It disappointed until it found its "killer application" with the smartphone, later that decade. And it was only with 4G that mobile networks actually lived up to the promises of 3G, such as being able to watch video streams. To really get the benefits that are promised for 5G, people may have to wait for 6G.

Mobile phones are more common than electricity in much of sub-Saharan Africa

A decade after mobile phones began to spread in Africa, they have become commonplace even in the continent's poorest countries. In 2016, two-fifths of people in sub-Saharan Africa had mobile phones. Their rapid spread has beaten all sorts of odds. In most African countries, less than half the population has access to electricity. In a third of those countries, less than a quarter does. Yet in much of the continent people with mobile phones outnumber those with electricity, despite the fact that they may have to walk for miles to get a signal or to recharge their phones' batteries.

A current problem

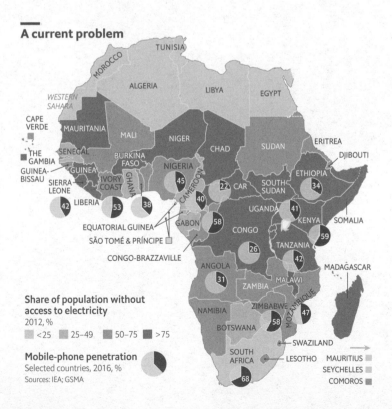

Share of population without access to electricity
2012, %
■ <25 ■ 25–49 ■ 50–75 ■ >75

Mobile-phone penetration
Selected countries, 2016, %
Sources: IEA; GSMA

Mobile phones have transformed the lives of hundreds of millions for whom they were the first, and often the only, way to connect with the outside world. They have made it possible for poor countries to leapfrog much more than landline telephony. Mobile-money services, which enable people to send cash straight from their phones, have in effect created personal bank accounts that people can carry in their pockets. By one estimate, the M-Pesa mobile-money system alone lifted about 2% of Kenyan households out of poverty between 2008 and 2014. Technology cannot solve all of Africa's problems, but it can help with some of them.

Why self-driving cars will mostly be shared, not owned

When will you be able to buy a driverless car that will work anywhere? This commonly asked question contains three assumptions: that autonomous vehicles (AVs) will resemble cars; that people will buy them; and that they will be capable of working on all roads in all conditions. All three of those assumptions may be wrong. Although today's experimental vehicles are modified versions of ordinary cars, with steering wheels that eerily turn by themselves, future AVs will have no steering wheel or pedals and will come in all sorts of shapes and sizes; pods capable of carrying six or eight people may prove to be the most efficient design. Rather than working everywhere, these pods will initially operate within geographically limited and well-mapped urban areas. And they will be shared "robotaxis", summoned when needed using a ride-hailing app. The first self-driving vehicle you ride in will be shared, not owned, for a combination of technological and economic reasons.

The technology needed to get vehicles to drive themselves has not yet been perfected, but it has improved enormously over the past decade and is on the verge of working reliably, at least in relatively simple urban environments with good weather. This explains why Phoenix, Arizona, is a popular place to test AVs; Waymo, the self-driving car unit of Google's parent company, hopes to launch a robotaxi service there by the end of 2018, based on Chrysler Pacifica minivans. Other robotaxi services will appear in the coming years in other cities, and the areas they cover will gradually be expanded. The initial deployment of self-driving vehicles as robotaxis makes sense because they only need to work within a particular area – and because the sensors needed for a fully autonomous AV to sense its surroundings and figure out how to respond currently cost more than the vehicle itself. That is less of a problem for a shared robotaxi, however, which will be in use and generating revenue for several hours a day. (Private cars, by contrast, are used on average only about 5% of the time.)

So economics and practicality dictate that AVs will start out as shared robotaxis. Eventually, perhaps by 2030 or so, the cost of sensors will fall and it will no longer be prohibitively expensive to buy your own self-driving vehicle. The question then is whether you would want to. For people living in cities, robotaxis could offer a far cheaper and more convenient alternative to car ownership. At the moment, travelling by Uber or another ride-hailing service costs around $2.50 a mile; but take away the driver, and that cost could fall to $0.70 a mile, reckon analysts at UBS, a bank. That is less than the $1.20 a mile it costs, on average, to run a private car (when fuel, insurance, servicing and other costs are factored in). So if robotaxis really work as advertised, many urbanites could ditch their cars and save thousands of dollars a year. UBS predicts that by 2035, 80% of people will use robotaxis in cities where they are available, and that urban car ownership will fall by 70%.

No doubt some people will still want to own a car, and will buy a self-driving one. But the total number of vehicles on the road will fall by about half from its current level, UBS predicts, and by 2050 those vehicles will be split roughly equally between robotaxis and privately owned AVs. The robotaxis, being in almost constant use, will account for the vast majority of miles travelled. With fewer private vehicles needing to be parked, vast swathes of land currently wasted on parking will be available for other uses, such as housing. As cars did in the 20th century, AVs will redefine retailing and reshape cities, as well as providing a convenient new form of mobility. As with cars, which lead to road deaths, pollution and congestion, there are likely to be unanticipated (and unpleasant) consequences for society from autonomous vehicles, such as a loss of privacy and the potential to use them as a means of social control. Removing the horse from horse-drawn carriages was an apparently simple change that had far-reaching effects. Similarly, there is much more to autonomous vehicles than simply removing the need for a driver – and much of their impact will be a consequence of the fact that they will mostly be shared, not owned.

How ride-hailing apps reduce drink-driving

Gun violence in America gets plenty of attention, but cars kill more people. Around 40,000 people a year die on American roads, more than all fatalities caused by firearms (of which two-thirds are suicides, not homicides). The death rate from motor accidents in America, around 12 people per 100,000, is more than twice that of western Europe. The grim toll of motor-vehicle deaths is widely seen as unavoidable, given that the United States is a large, sprawling country primarily designed around the automobile. But around a third of these deaths has involved drunk drivers, suggesting that there is, in fact, substantial room for improvement. Indeed, it appears that the advent of ride-hailing apps like Uber and Lyft has had a welcome impact on road safety.

According to a working paper by Jessica Lynn Peck of the Graduate Centre at the City University of New York, the arrival of Uber in New York City may have helped reduce alcohol-related traffic accidents by 25–35%, as people opt to hail a ride home after a night out, rather than driving themselves. Uber was first introduced in the city in May 2011, but did not spread through the rest of the state. The study uses this as a natural experiment. To control for factors unrelated to Uber's launch, such as adverse weather conditions, Ms Peck compares accident rates in each of New York's five boroughs to those in the counties where Uber was not present, picking those that had the most similar population density and pre-2011 drunk-driving rate.

The four boroughs which were quick to adopt Uber – Manhattan, Brooklyn, Queens and the Bronx – all saw decreases in alcohol-related car crashes relative to their lookalike counties. By contrast, Staten Island, where Uber caught on more slowly, saw no such decrease. It should not take ride-hailing apps to curb drunk driving, but any reduction is worth hailing.

Worth hailing

Alcohol-related crashes in New York City

Difference* in the number of crashes in boroughs when compared with similar counties

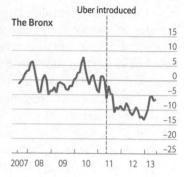

The Bronx

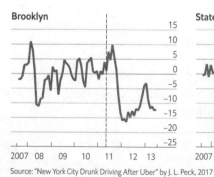

Queens

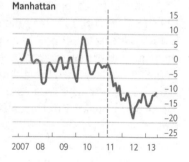

Manhattan

Brooklyn

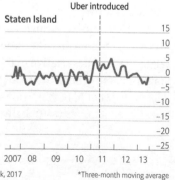

Staten Island

Source: "New York City Drunk Driving After Uber" by J. L. Peck, 2017

*Three-month moving average

What is augmented reality?

Most people, by now, have heard of virtual reality (VR). Giant technology companies, from Google to Samsung to Sony, are hoping that it will be the next big hit in consumer electronics, though it has failed to break out of a specialist niche. Its close cousin, augmented reality (AR), is less well known. Yet many people think that AR, when it comes, could have a much bigger impact than VR ever will. What exactly is it?

The first thing to realise is that "reality" means two almost entirely different things depending on which technology you are talking about. VR aims to generate an immersive artificial reality: a convincing computer simulation of the world for its users to explore. AR, on the other hand, sticks with "real" reality, and uses computers to layer useful or interesting information on top of it. That is not a new idea. AR's early ancestors include the heads-up displays that were fitted to jet fighters starting in the 1950s, projecting information about airspeed, heading and the like directly onto the cockpit glass. Many people with smartphones will have had experience of more advanced versions. Snapchat, a messaging app, is famous for its ability to doctor photos of faces to give people rabbit ears, baseball caps, improbable moustaches and so on. Pokemon Go, a popular smartphone game, uses AR to superimpose virtual creatures onto the real world. Users of Google's Translate app can point their phones at street signs and menus written in foreign languages, and see the text magically translated into their native tongue.

But AR's proponents want to go much further than that. Their goal is to develop "smart glasses" that can project three-dimensional images in the user's field of vision that appear to blend perfectly into the real world. For now, the firm that has made the most progress is Microsoft. Its HoloLens headset is a self-contained computer that uses a suite of sensors to build a 3D model of the world around it. It can then do everything from placing a set of virtual "Minecraft" blocks onto a kitchen table to generating virtual cadavers for anatomy students to study. Other companies are interested, too. Magic Leap, a startup based in Florida, has attracted $2.3bn in investment to develop a similar technology. Facebook, which bought Oculus, a VR company, for $2bn in 2014, says its ultimate goal is to produce a set of glasses that can do both VR and AR at the same time.

For now, that is a long way off. The HoloLens is impressive, but it is just an early incarnation of the technology, which can be expected to improve rapidly in the coming years, just as the brick-like mobile phones of the 1980s evolved into modern smartphones. And for AR to take off as a consumer technology, inventors will need to solve more than just technical problems. Social factors matter, too. What is the right etiquette if you are talking to someone and a text message pops into your field of vision? Will wearing smart glasses at the dining table, or in a meeting, be considered impolite? Most technology analysts think AR will make its first inroads in the workplace, where social mores are less important. Smart glasses can help a technician identify a component that needs to be replaced, for example, or give a surgeon the illusion of being able to see inside a patient during an operation. VR lets you escape into a different reality. But because AR is used in the real world, it could have many more benefits – and is also likely to have unexpected social consequences.

Why we're still waiting for the space elevator

For decades, engineers and science-fiction writers have dreamed of lifts capable of carrying things into orbit from the Earth's surface. Konstantin Tsiolkovsky, a Russian scientist, suggested the idea in 1895, inspired by the Eiffel Tower. And in 1979 Arthur C. Clarke wrote an entire novel, *The Fountains of Paradise*, about the construction of such a space elevator. Thanks to SpaceX and other private spaceflight companies, rocket launches have fallen in price in recent years. Each launch of the Falcon Heavy, the most powerful rocket in operation today, costs around $90m. But whisking satellites, space probes and even people into orbit on a giant elevator might be cheaper, more reliable and more civilised than using giant fireworks – if one could be built. Unfortunately, the technical challenges are formidable.

The basic idea of a space elevator is to run a fixed cable from a point on the Earth's equator to a space station directly overhead, in geostationary orbit (that is, at an altitude of 36,000km). Objects at that altitude circle the planet once a day, so they have the useful characteristic of appearing to hover over a fixed spot on the Earth's surface. Cargo-carrying vehicles can then be run up and down the cable. They need to be powered on the way up, but can reclaim energy as gravity helps them on the way down. These vehicles would have to be quite large to carry people: even if they moved at 500kph, the trip in each direction would take three days. And building a 36,000km-long high-speed railway on Earth would be hard enough. Building a vertical one into space would be much more difficult.

The chief obstacle is that no known material has the necessary combination of lightness and strength needed for the cable, which has to be able to support its own weight. Carbon nanotubes are often touted as a possibility, but they have only about a tenth of the necessary strength-to-weight ratio and cannot be made into filaments more than a few centimetres long, let alone thousands of kilometres. Diamond nanothreads, another exotic form of carbon, might be stronger, but their properties are still poorly understood. Even if a suitable material could be found, the part of the cable within the atmosphere would be subject to weather disturbances, and the vehicles running up and down it could also cause dangerous oscillations. Anchoring it to a moveable, seagoing platform might help, but keeping the cable steady would still be a tall order. A further worry is collisions: there are thousands of satellites and other items in orbit around the Earth, from an altitude of around 2,000km upwards. Any impact with the cable could cause disaster.

True believers in space elevators continue to look for ways around these problems, but they may be insurmountable. The idea refuses to die, however, possibly because of its elegance and simplicity. Perhaps the dream will be realised, just not on Earth. Building a space elevator between the moon's surface and lunar orbit (to transport things such as visiting tourists or material mined on the moon) would be far easier, because of the weaker gravity and lack of atmosphere. Anyone hoping to take a space elevator into orbit from Earth, however, faces a long wait.

How astronomers spotted the first interstellar asteroid

On October 19th 2017 Rob Weryk of the University of Hawaii saw something rather strange. In pictures produced by Pan-STARRS 1, a telescope on Haleakala, he identified an unusually fast-moving, faint object that he concluded could not have originated in Earth's solar system. It was travelling at more than 25km per second. That is too fast for it to have a closed, elliptical orbit around the Sun. Nor could its velocity have been the result of the extra gravitational kick provided by an encounter with a planet, since the object arrived from well above the ecliptic plane near which all the Sun's planets orbit. Indeed, after swinging around the Sun, it passed about 25m km below Earth, before speeding back above the ecliptic plane. Observations from other telescopes confirmed that Dr Weryk's object was the first extrasolar object to be spied by astronomers within our own solar system.

The object was originally classified as a comet and thus named C/2017 U1 (the "C" stands for comet). But it lacked the tail of gas and dust produced when such icy rocks fly close to the Sun. Furthermore, an analysis of the sunlight it reflected suggested that its surface was reddish, and was mostly rock. So it was first reclassified as an asteroid, A/2017 U1. Then, once its interstellar origin had been confirmed, it was renamed 1I/2017 U1. It was also given a proper name: 'Oumuamua, from a Hawaiian word meaning "scout". Measurements of its brightness suggest that it is a cigar-shaped object, about 230 metres long and 35 metres wide, tumbling end over end. Its rocky nature is puzzling. Comets are formed on the cold periphery of distant solar systems. Asteroids reside within such systems' interiors, where any comet-like volatiles will have been driven off by the heat of their parent stars. Models of planet formation suggest that interstellar objects are more likely to be comets, as they can be more easily dislodged from their orbits than asteroids.

One possible explanation is that over many millennia, as 1I/2017

U1 travelled between the stars, cosmic rays might have transformed the icy, volatile chemicals that would be expected to stream off a comet into more stable compounds. Another is that the Sun is not the first star 1I/2017 U1 has chanced upon, and its volatile materials have been boiled off by previous stellar encounters. Or it could indeed be that the object was rocky to begin with – perhaps once orbiting its parent star in an equivalent of our solar system's asteroid belt, before its ejection by an encounter with a Jupiter-like planet.

Why, then, has nothing like 1I/2017 U1 been seen before? Those planet-formation theories suggest such objects should be a reasonably common sight. Perhaps the theories are wrong. Or perhaps these interstellar visitors have been overlooked in the past, and 1I/2017 U1 will now inspire a spate of such sightings in future. Sadly for astronomers, it may not be visible long enough for these questions to be resolved decisively. It is now charging out of the solar system towards the constellation of Pegasus – at 44km per second. Small uncertainties in the calculation of its trajectory may mean that where exactly it came from and where it is heading will remain a mystery. But of its interstellar origin there is no doubt.

Why drones could pose a greater risk to aircraft than birds

The "Miracle on the Hudson" – the successful ditching of a US Airways jetliner into New York's Hudson River in 2009 after it hit a flock of geese – taught frequent flyers two things. First, it really is possible to land an aircraft on water, just as is shown on seat-back safety cards (at least for a small, narrow-body jet). Second, and more worryingly, the incident showed how dangerous birds can be to aircraft, particularly when they get sucked into engines. Aircraft engines are supposed to be designed to withstand an impact by the feathered creatures. Using big guns, chickens have been fired at aircraft engines in safety tests since the 1950s. More recently, that has prompted another question. If birds can be so dangerous, what about drones?

New research suggests that small unmanned aerial vehicles (UAVs) might actually do more damage than birds at the same impact speed, even if they are a similar weight. The study, published by the Alliance for System Safety of Unmanned Aerial Systems in conjunction with Research Excellence, a think-tank, used computer simulations to examine the impact of bird and drone collisions with planes in more than 180 scenarios. The researchers found that the drones' rigid and dense materials – such as metal, plastic and lithium batteries – can put planes at much greater risk than the relatively squishy body of a bird. Kiran D'Souza, one of the authors, says that in every collision scenario with a drone there was at least minor damage to the plane – and sometimes it was much more severe. In one case, the researchers discovered that if a drone were to hit an aircraft engine's fan blades when it is operating at its highest speed, the blades could shatter, causing the engine to fail.

These findings paint a grim picture, given that in the past two years the number of drone sightings by pilots has surged. According to the Federal Aviation Administration (FAA), there are around 100 cases each month of drones potentially endangering an aircraft, and two collisions have already happened in North America. In

September 2017 a drone collided with a helicopter near Staten Island in New York, and the following month an aircraft was struck by a drone in Québec City. Both aircraft landed safely, but given the regulations in place, neither UAV should have been flying in the first place. In America drones are required to stay in sight of their pilot, which was not the case with the helicopter collision. They also must fly at or below 400 feet and yield to manned aircraft. In Canada UAVs are not allowed to operate above 300 feet, and airports, helipads and seaplane bases are considered "No Drone Zones". Europe has also seen at least three aircraft collisions with drones since 2010, and has been conducting research to examine the dangers.

With so many drone-owners flouting the rules, some experts think that it is just luck that a serious collision has not yet happened. America's FAA says it is working to create new regulations to reduce the risks drones pose to planes. New safety standards for engines may be needed to make them more resistant to impacts with the flying contraptions. In addition, existing regulations on where drones can and cannot fly should be more strictly policed. The FAA is also looking to UAV-makers and users to develop detect-and-avoid technology to prevent collisions with each other, and with manned aircraft. Given the millions of travellers who take to the sky each day, efforts to keep them safe will surely have to come from both sides.

What is the point of spam e-mail?

According to internet folklore, the very first spam e-mail was sent in 1978, to around 400 recipients. The sender was given a ticking-off, and told not to do it again. Alas for that golden age. These days, a torrent of e-mails littered with misspellings promising to cure wrinkles, enlarge penises, banish fat or wire millions in unclaimed offshore wealth is the fate of almost everyone with an e-mail address. Other e-mails aim to harvest usernames and passwords, or contain deceptive links to malicious software designed to take over a user's computer. According to one estimate from SecureList, a cyber-security firm, roughly 60% of all e-mail is spam. But why? What is the point of the avalanche of spam?

In a word, money. Spam is the digital cousin of ordinary, paper-based junk mail. Firms send this out because they think it will drum up business. By reducing the cost of communication, the internet turbocharges that business model. Real-world junk mail might be profitable if only one recipient in a thousand decides she needs double-glazed windows or a greasy pizza. But sending an e-mail is far cheaper than sending a piece of paper. With a list of address and the right software, thousands of messages can be sent every hour. And because internet users do not pay by the message, the marginal cost per message is essentially zero. All this means that even if only one recipient in a million is conned into buying some dubious pills or clicking a link that reveals their credit-card details, the revenues far outweigh the costs.

The relative anonymity offered by the internet also enables spammers to hide their identities, which allows more obviously criminal uses of e-mail. Phishing e-mails, which try to persuade users to enter sensitive details such as banking passwords into fake (but convincing-looking) websites, can be very profitable, because the data they harvest can allow their controllers to loot bank accounts or go on buying sprees with stolen credit-card information. Malicious attachments can subvert a user's machine, perhaps recruiting it into a "botnet", a horde of compromised machines that can be rented out to attackers to knock websites offline. And then there is "ransomware", in which a malicious program encrypts all the files on the victim's computer, then displays instructions demanding payment to unscramble them. All this is made possible by giant lists of e-mail addresses that are bought, sold and swapped between spammers. Those, in turn, are generated from leaks, hacks, guesswork and addresses collected from users of shady websites and subsequently sold on.

Busts are not unheard of (a big Nigerian spammer, believed to be behind thousands of online scams earning more than $60m, was arrested in August 2016). But they are not common enough to put a meaningful dent in the business. Instead, computer firms such as Microsoft and Google have become locked in an arms race with the spammers. Spam filters began appearing in the 1990s, as the internet gained mainstream popularity. Spammers altered their tactics to work around them (which is why spam is full of deliberate misspellings such as "v1agr*"). For now, tech firms have the advantage: artificial-intelligence filters can be trained to recognise the characteristics of spam messages, and reroute them to spam folders. Training those filters requires them to have plenty of recent examples to practise on. With spam, at least, that is not a problem.

Why the police should wear body cameras

Grainy footage of police officers shooting members of the public has become unhappily familiar in recent years. Smartphones, which have proliferated, enable anyone to record police actions. The footage of the death of Keith Lamont Scott, which prompted violent protests in North Carolina in September 2016, was striking for another reason – it came from the police. It is increasingly common for police officers to sport a camera on their uniforms. A growing body of evidence suggests that the gadgets improve the behaviour both of cops and those they deal with.

A study published in 2016 by researchers at the University of Cambridge and RAND Europe, a think-tank, suggested that body cameras can slash the number of complaints made about the police. Over the course of a year, around 2,000 officers in two forces in America and four in Britain were randomly assigned cameras according to their shift. Compared with the previous year, the number of complaints brought against them dropped by 93%. The number of complaints also fell when officers were not wearing cameras during the trial, an effect the authors call "contagious accountability". According to Barak Ariel, one of the researchers on the Cambridge study, officers who wore cameras but only started recording in the middle of their interactions with the public were more likely to use force than those not using them. So for the best results, police officers should have little or no discretion in when to turn the cameras on or off.

Civil-liberty campaigners welcome the chance to keep an eye on the police. Many police forces are enthusiastic too. Dealing with complaints is expensive. Cameras also improve the behaviour of members of the public and reduce the number of bogus complaints brought against the police. They are an efficient way to collect evidence. They can be used in training; officers can learn from their colleagues' actions. Mr Ariel reckons British cops are more open to the devices than their American counterparts. Police unions in Boston and Cincinnati say they should not be rolled out until their contracts are changed to reflect the new work that cameras will demand.

Yet the use of cameras brings new challenges. If police record every interaction with the public, they will have to find a way to store the many hours of footage generated. Questions will then arise as to how long such data should be kept and in what circumstances recordings should be released to the public. Such worries are not insignificant. But the evidence is mounting that the usefulness of such cameras outweighs the drawbacks.

Why tech giants are laying their own undersea cables

In September 2017 Microsoft and Facebook announced the completion of a 6,600km (4,100-mile) cable stretching from Virginia Beach, Virginia, to Bilbao, Spain. Dubbed Marea, Spanish for "tide", the bundle of eight fibre-optic threads, roughly the size of a garden hose, is the highest-capacity connection across the Atlantic Ocean. It is capable of transferring 160 terabits of data every second, the equivalent of more than 5,000 high-resolution movies.

Such ultra-fast fibre networks are needed to keep up with the torrent of data flowing around the world. In 2016 international bandwidth usage reached 3,544 terabits per second, roughly double the figure in 2014. Firms such as Google, Facebook and Microsoft used to lease all their international bandwidth from carriers such as BT or AT&T. Now they need so much network capacity to synchronise data across their networks of data centres around the world that it makes more sense to lay their own dedicated cables.

This has led to a boom in new undersea cable systems. The

Plumbing the depths
Active and planned submarine cable systems owned* by:
October 2017

— Facebook — Google — Microsoft — Other

Marea

Source:
TeleGeography

*In full
or in part

Submarine Telecoms Forum, an industry body, reckons that 100,000km of submarine cable was laid in 2016, up from just 16,000km in 2015. TeleGeography, a market-research firm, reckons that $9.2bn will have been spent on such cable projects between 2016 and 2018, five times as much as in the previous three years.

Game theory: sport and leisure

Why tennis players grunt

It has become common behaviour in top-level tennis, like the pumped fist on winning a set and the expletive aimed at a coach after an error. "Grunting" is too limited a name for it. The noises made by modern tennis professionals range from wounded roars to frantic shrieks. Gone are the days of hushed rallies, punctuated only by the thwack of felt on strings. Like sledging in cricket (talking to an opponent to disturb their concentration) and bat-flipping in baseball (throwing the bat in the air after a sizeable hit), squealing in tennis is considered by some players and spectators to be a blight on the game.

All three vices have been around for decades. Tennis's best-known early grunters were Jimmy Connors and John McEnroe. Stars of the 1970s and the 1980s, and hardly famed for their courtesy on court, they used to groan with ostentatious exertion. Yet if they could claim to be exhaling with effort during particularly strenuous rallies, then Monica Seles extended the practice. In the 1990s she pioneered stroke-by-stroke screeches, delivered apparently regardless of exertion. Ms Seles is one of several successful whiners to have been trained by Nick Bollettieri, an American coach, along with Andre Agassi, the Williams sisters and Maria Sharapova. Mr Bollettieri claims that the tactic is "a release of energy in a constructive way". At more than 100 decibels, Ms Sharapova's wailing is, briefly, almost as loud as a chainsaw or helicopter. Rafael Nadal is another bellower, to the irritation of his rival, Roger Federer. But even the GOAT (the "Greatest Of All Time", as Mr Federer's fans call him) has been known to bray under duress.

Grunting in tennis has been shown to give the player responsible a definite advantage. Two separate studies of college players have found that the speed of their serves and ground-strokes increased by 4–5% when they groaned. The authors of both papers note that similar gains in performance have been observed in noisy weightlifters and martial artists. The most likely cause is the extra tension created in the athlete's core muscles by the grunt. The pitch of the grunt also seems relevant. An analysis of 50 fixtures featuring some of the world's top 30 players demonstrated that the men hollered a semitone higher in matches that they lost, and that the difference in pitch was clear from early in the contest. It was unclear, however, whether this change was a cause or effect of the poorer performance. Players seeking further reason to unlock their inner grunter should also note the effects of the sounds on their opponents. An experiment which required subjects to guess the direction of tennis shots on a video screen found that an accompanying burst of white noise hampered their reaction times. It took them an extra 30 milliseconds to read the direction of the ball, during which it would typically travel two feet. The participants were merely recreational players, but professionals may be even more reliant on sound, because they can use it to guess the spin on the ball.

With such compelling proof of grunting's benefits, and so much to be gained from winning – the total prize money for a grand slam is typically $40m–50m – it is remarkable that there are any silent rallies at all. A crackdown on excessive exhaling seems unlikely. Rumours of an on-court "gruntometer" to establish a maximum volume faded five years ago. Umpires are allowed to award points against a player who causes an opponent a "deliberate hindrance", but rarely do so. "Quiet please", their favourite instruction, applies only to the crowd. For the foreseeable future, tennis fans will have to put up with the unseemly racket.

Why board games are so popular in Nigeria

When it comes to Scrabble, Nigerians rule the board. In November 2017, they retained the team title at the world championships in Nairobi. Nigeria boasts more top-100 players than any other country. But the impact of board games in Africa's most populous country goes beyond these world-class Scrabble-masters. Board games are played across Nigeria, from indigenous games like *ayo* that make use of counters or pebbles (mancala is a similar game in the United States), to chess and Monopoly.

It is impossible to quantify how many Nigerians play board games, but there is no doubt that they are more popular in the better-educated south. Prince Anthony Ikolo, the coach of Nigeria's national Scrabble team, estimates that 4,000 Scrabblers play in more than 100 clubs around the country (compared with around 2,000–2,500 members in 152 clubs in America and Canada combined). The Niger Delta states and Lagos are home to many of the country's Scrabble champions. Wellington Jighere, who won the world championship in 2015, is from the oil-rich city of Warri, which is particularly renowned for producing world-class players.

On the national tournament circuit, cash prizes can reach $10,000. Prestigious schools have chess and Scrabble teams, and there are also university tournaments. Lagos, the country's teeming commercial capital, got its own Monopoly board in 2012. The property-buying game was made an official sport in Lagos state in 2016. In September that year, more than 1,200 students competed for the top prize of a 600,000 naira ($1,700) education grant. In the process, they broke the world record for the number of students playing Monopoly.

Board games are mainly a middle-class pursuit, although Ludo, draughts and their ilk are also popular among the less educated. Many Nigerians have a competitive streak: the country's unofficial motto, "Naija no dey carry last", can be roughly translated as "Nigerians strive to finish first." Those with an intellectual bent may therefore relish challenging others at Monopoly or Scrabble.

Many say their skills were nurtured during long holidays and evenings without regular electricity, by parents who were keen for their offspring to spend time "IQ building" rather than idling. Board games also allow Nigerians to focus on something other than the daily *wahala*, a word for trouble or stress (be it watching the hours tick by in urban traffic jams, appeasing a corrupt policeman or finding the money to keep the family generator running). And in a country where millions of Evangelical Christians follow a prosperity gospel and wealth is often idolised, Monopoly can temporarily allow Nigerians to indulge their fantasies.

How drones can keep beaches safe from sharks

Australia's waters are some of the most dangerous in the world. Ignoring, for a moment, the dangers posed by jellyfish and salt-water crocodiles, the average annual number of so-called "unprovoked" shark attacks more than doubled between 1990–2000 and 2005–2015, to 15. One company in Western Australia has a futuristic solution. Shark Alert International has equipped a drone with military-grade cameras that can "x-ray" the water, then send alerts to lifeguards and even surfers' watches. The technology was originally designed to help America detect a different foe: Russian submarines. It sees deep into the water by taking images at several different optical frequencies every second. In tests in California, the company said that it could spot dummy sharks 15 feet (4.6 metres) beneath the surface with total accuracy. The cameras might work at twice that depth in Perth's clear waters.

Helicopters and low-flying planes have long patrolled popular beaches. Yet human spotters are expensive and often ineffectual because not all sharks swim near the surface. Choppy waters and bright reflections make them difficult to spot when they do. Drones are cheaper, can hover over beaches constantly, and have already been tested in some parts of the country. In New South Wales, another hotspot for attacks, researchers have also combined drones with software able to identify sharks. The drones feed live videos through a system that is taught how to differentiate sharks from surfers and boats with far greater accuracy than the human eye. Messages can be relayed to lifeguards and emergency services, while megaphones attached to the drones blast out warnings when a dangerous species is spotted.

Politicians are buying into other high-tech solutions as well. One involves the modification of drum-lines, which hang baited hooks between a buoy and the ocean floor, to catch sharks that might otherwise swim towards the beaches. Some new versions of the hooks can alert officials when they snag a shark, allowing the fish to be tagged, towed and released far away in deeper waters.

Scientists using these "smart" drum-lines in northern Brazil reported a 97% decline in attacks. After a young surfer was killed in April 2017, Western Australia's Labor government subsidised 1,000 personal deterrent devices called Shark Shields, which emit an electromagnetic field supposed to ward off attacks. Researchers are also experimenting with camouflaged wetsuits that seem to deter nibbles, and "counter-illumination" surfboards whose undersides emit light to diminish their silhouette. Some scientists worry about public splurges on such technologies. The Shark Shield, for example, may deter some "investigative" attacks, but has no effect on the ambushes to which surfers may fall victim. And sharks still perish on the smart drum-lines that are supposed to save them.

Culling, however, is even worse. Many shark species, including the great white, are protected in Australia. But politicians can seek exemptions, and numerous beaches are still guarded by nets and conventional drum-lines. These methods kill other, often endangered, species too. New South Wales snagged 133 "target" sharks in meshes along its northern coast between 2015 and 2016, as well as 615 other animals. And because shark attacks are so uncommon, the evidence for the effectiveness of the methods used to limit them is thin. The increase in shark attacks could be the result of an increase in the size of Australia's shark populations after decades of conservation. But a bigger factor is likely to be the larger number of humans in the water. Once larger populations of sharks and humans are taken into account, today's swimmers are actually safer than ever. With or without swanky new solutions, the risks of meeting a toothy end are microscopic.

How football transfers work

In football, July and August are known as the "silly season" – and looking at Neymar's record-breaking €222m ($261m) move from Barcelona to Paris Saint-Germain (PSG) in 2017, it is easy to see why. The two months form the summer transfer window in which football teams are allowed to buy each other's players. With few competitive club games to enjoy, fans turn their attention to gossiping about exciting arrivals and unwanted departures. Neymar was both. PSG had been trying to prise the Brazilian star from Catalonia for months. The saga reached a ridiculous crescendo as his Barcelona teammates insisted on social media that he was staying, while newspapers told of his imminent departure, which was confirmed on August 3rd. Barcelona complained that PSG's Qatari owners financed the purchase, rather than using the club's revenues, which would breach the rules: teams are only allowed to spend as much as they earn. But as television revenues and sponsorship contracts have fattened, so have transfer fees. Most elite sides are willing to spend upwards of €40m on a talented addition to their squad. How do they arrange such deals?

Before anybody gets to the negotiating table, the buying team will have spent years identifying the right asset. Clubs have long relied on scouts to spot gifted youngsters, but they also have access to enormous video libraries and troves of performance data. Though the manager is usually involved in choosing the target, the haggling is often done by a "director of football" or senior executive. If the player is under contract at another club, the executive must make a formal approach to that team. There are rules that prevent the buyer from contacting the player or his agent beforehand, an underhand practice known as "tapping up". Nonetheless, rumours of interest from either party are often leaked to the press.

The subsequent negotiations are mostly conducted via WhatsApp, a mobile-messaging service, says Jake Cohen, a sports lawyer: its group-chat function, instant updates and security make it particularly convenient. Several agreements have to be thrashed out before a transfer can be completed. The first deal concerns the fee that the vendors will receive. Some players, such as Neymar, have a release clause – a sum that his owners have to accept, in his case €222m. Once the selling club feels that the price is about right, the second stage begins: the buying team offers a contract to the player via his agent, which for Neymar meant an annual package of €30m after tax. The third settlement is the commission that the purchasing club pays the player's agent, which is typically 5–10% of the transfer fee, according to Andrew McGregor of Brabners, a law firm. Neymar's team of representatives, which included his father, pocketed a more generous reward of €38m. After putting its new player through a rigorous medical examination and filing the paperwork with the right regulatory bodies, the buying club can announce the signing.

If that seems complicated, it is made trickier still by fiddly clauses. The selling club might demand future payments if the player wins a trophy, or makes another lucrative move. The buyer will offer him performance bonuses, and compensation for using his image if he is a celebrity. Above all, the leverage lies with the footballer himself. If his contract expires, he is allowed to walk away – a disastrous loss for his old team and a windfall for his new one, which will reward him with a cut of the avoided transfer fee. As the price of a lethal striker or a robust defender spirals, expect to see more players holding their owners to ransom.

How St Louis became America's chess capital

St Louis is a troubled, shrinking city in the American Midwest. Its population peaked at 850,000 in the 1950s. Decades of middle-class flight have left it with only 315,000 residents, of which almost one-third live at or below the federal poverty level. It has America's highest per-capita murder rate and remains one of its most segregated cities. In 2014 riots erupted in Ferguson, a suburb, after a white police officer fatally shot a black teenager. It therefore seems an unlikely candidate to be a mecca for chess. Yet in May 2013, the United States Congress declared St Louis the chess capital of the country. How did this happen?

The rise of St Louis as a centre for chess dates back to 2008, when Rex Sinquefield chose the promotion of chess in his home town as a retirement project after making a fortune pioneering stockmarket index funds. (Mr Sinquefield is also politically active as a campaigner for the abolition of income tax and a sponsor of right-wing think-tanks.) In 2008 he founded the Chess Club and Scholastic Centre of St Louis, which has since become the headquarters of American chess. The 6,000-sq-ft centre includes a hall for tournaments, classrooms, a library and play areas. Some 1,000 members of all skill levels attend classes such as "Pure Beginners Ladies' Knight". In 2011 Mr Sinquefield helped bring the "World Chess Hall of Fame" to St Louis. It was set up, according to its website, "to educate visitors, fans, players and scholars by collecting, preserving, exhibiting and interpreting the game of chess and its continuing cultural and artistic significance".

Mr Sinquefield's perseverance paid off. The club began hosting the American championship, the nation's top tournament, in 2009, bringing grandmasters galore to the city. (Before that it was held in different cities.) The Sinquefield tournament, set up by its eponymous benefactor, started in 2013 with a prize fund of $170,000. It attracts the world's top players and was watched by some 1.5m online viewers in 2016. Several universities in the St Louis area now offer chess scholarships; Wesley So, the world number two, attended the city's Webster University on one such scholarship. Local high schools, including in and around Ferguson, promote after-school classes. In 2017 Webster University won the national championship at the President's Cup collegiate chess tournament in New York for the fifth time in a row. St Louis University finished third.

The revival of chess in St Louis has helped make America one of the world's top chess nations again. In 2008 no American was in the top ten players, according to the World Chess Federation (The first American on the list appeared at in 17th place.) By 2017 three of the top ten players in the world (numbers two, four and seven) were American. Indeed, one of them, Fabiano Caruana, moved to St Louis in 2015.

What does "digitally remastering" a film really mean?

In April 2017 Rialto Pictures and Studiocanal released *The Graduate* (1967) in a "new digital print" in honour of the film's 50th anniversary. A 2016 version of *Dr Strangelove* (1964) boasts a "restored 4K digital transfer". *Citizen Kane* (1941) "dazzles anew" in a "superb 75th-anniversary high-definition" digital restoration. Most film buffs understand these terms to be vaguely synonymous with improvement. But what does the process of "restoration" and "remastering" involve? And is it necessary, or just a ruse to sell old movies in new packaging?

Until the 1990s, movies were made exclusively with analogue cameras and photosensitive film. These produce an image as light streams through the lens and turns microscopic crystals into silver forms – which can then be developed into a permanent (and even colourful) picture, using chemicals in a darkroom. The resulting frame is highly detailed, but also susceptible to flaws. Temperature changes, dirt or rough handling can introduce stains or a grainy texture. Digital cinematography avoids these problems: an image-sensor chip converts the scene into millions of pixels, each of which is a miniature square with a numerically coded brightness and colour. Most modern movies are made and distributed this way. It allows directors to review takes immediately, lets editors enhance them on computers and enables studios to send them to cinemas without shipping hefty reels around the world. Some purists demur, because analogue film can still produce a higher resolution.

Viewers aren't as picky, and almost all consume video digitally. Whether they are streaming *Casablanca* (1942) or watching *The Godfather* (1972) on Blu-ray (a more capacious format than DVDs), they are served a scan of the original 35mm film. The studio has converted each physical image into pixels. A full restoration and remastering of a film, however, goes a step further. The film roll is cleaned, to remove dust. Technicians then work frame by frame to restore the film, removing interference (such as noise, scratches and other signs of ageing), enhancing colours and sharpening outlines. Additional special effects and CGI may also be added. The audio will be overhauled at this stage, too, and perhaps remixed to introduce surround sound. The process is laborious, usually taking more than a year to complete.

Such painstaking adjustments are easy to miss without looking at a side-by-side comparison. Fans tend to focus instead on tweaks to the action, because some directors cannot resist tinkering with the story as well as the image. George Lucas, who pioneered the use of digital cameras in the *Star Wars* prequels at the beginning of the 21st century, upset fans by adding new scenes and editing dialogue in the original *Star Wars* trilogy when it was remastered in 1997. DVDs of Ridley Scott's *Blade Runner* (1982) boast of a "futuristic vision perfected", partly because of the improved special effects, but also thanks to a changed ending. There are other risks: though reels of film decay and are easy to lose, they can preserve a film for decades, whereas the longevity of digital media is less certain. And heavy-handed remastering risks losing some of the qualities that made these films so special in the first place.

How bookmakers deal with winning customers

888, an online betting firm, was fined a record £7.8m ($10.3m) in August 2017 after more than 7,000 vulnerable customers, who had disabled their betting accounts in an effort to prevent themselves from gambling, were still able to access their accounts. Yet away from the regulator's gaze, bookies often stand accused of the opposite excess: being too prompt to shun winning customers. Successful bettors complain that their accounts get closed down for what are sometimes described as business decisions. Others say their wagers get capped overnight to minuscule amounts. The move may be unpopular with punters, but in most parts of the world it is legal.

Bookmakers say scrutinising winners is necessary to help prevent fraud. Competition in the gambling industry increased with the arrival of online betting, prompting bookmakers to offer odds on markets they did not previously cover. In some, such as eastern European football leagues, low wages and late payments make fertile ground for match-fixing. A winning streak at the windows can signal foul play. Most often, however, efforts to spot savvy customers are not rooted in a desire to thwart dodgy schemes. Rather, they are part of what industry insiders call "risk management": to remain profitable, bookies seek to cap potential losses. As one betting consultant puts it, "Bookmakers close unprofitable accounts, just as insurance companies will not cover houses that are prone to flooding". Betting outlets get to know their customers by gleaning information online, tracking web habits and checking whether punters visit odds-comparison sites. Profiling has also been made easier by the tightening of anti-money-laundering regulations, which require online punters to provide detailed information when opening accounts.

Bookmakers argue that such screening is needed to restrict their involvement with professional gamblers. That in turn allows them to offer better odds to ordinary punters. Critics retort that the net is being cast too widely. Bookies may spend considerable resources trying to spot those who bet for a living, many of whom hire quantitative analysts to estimate outcomes and develop hedging strategies (in some cases seeking to exploit discrepancies between odds offered by several bookmakers to make a guaranteed profit). Online bookmakers respond with sophisticated algorithms that flag customers betting odd amounts of money – £13.04, say – on the basis that ordinary punters usually wager round sums. They take a closer look at those who snub free bets or bonuses, which rarely fit professional bettors' models and come with terms and conditions attached. They scrutinise user behaviour. While casual punters are more likely to bet minutes before an event begins, pros will often seek the best odds by laying their wager days in advance (because the longer one waits to bet, the more information becomes available about a particular event, and thus the easier it is for bookmakers to price it). And they look at customers' tendencies to win, sometimes accepting bets at a loss if a punter, seemingly acting on inside knowledge, allows them to gain market intelligence.

This explains why professional gamblers rarely do business with high-street bookmakers. They often place their trades on betting exchanges like Betfair or Smarkets, which do not restrict winning customers (though Betfair charges a premium to some of its most successful users). Alternatively, they work with those bookmakers who use successful gamblers to improve the efficiency of their betting markets, and make most of their money on commission. These profess not to limit winning accounts and accept much bigger bets (Pinnacle, an influential bookie, often has a $1m limit for major events). Betting professionals also sneak in big trades via brokers, like Gambit Research, a British operation that uses technology to place multiple smaller bets with a range of bookmakers. Asian agents, in particular, have made their names in that trade: many are able to channel sizeable bets to local bookies anonymously. Unlike the sports they love, the games played by professional gamblers and bookmakers are kept out of the spotlight.

The world's highest-earning football clubs

Manchester United retained their title as football's highest-earning club when Deloitte, a consultancy, released its annual Football Money League rankings in January 2018. The Red Devils failed to qualify for the 2016–17 season of the lucrative Champions League, and had to settle for winning the Europa League, a second-tier international club competition. Nonetheless, even though the club's success on the pitch paled in comparison with that of Real Madrid, who won both the Champions League and Spain's La Liga,

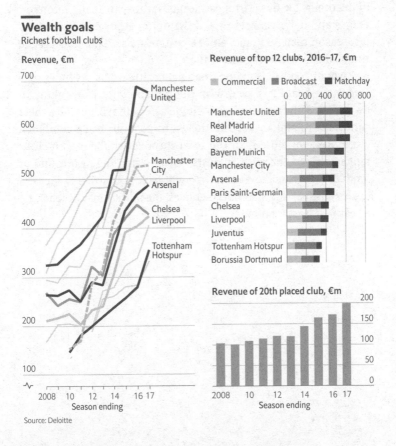

Wealth goals
Richest football clubs

Revenue, €m

Manchester United
Manchester City
Arsenal
Chelsea
Liverpool
Tottenham Hotspur

Season ending

Revenue of top 12 clubs, 2016–17, €m

Commercial ■ Broadcast ■ Matchday

Manchester United
Real Madrid
Barcelona
Bayern Munich
Manchester City
Arsenal
Paris Saint-Germain
Chelsea
Liverpool
Juventus
Tottenham Hotspur
Borussia Dortmund

Revenue of 20th placed club, €m

Season ending

Source: Deloitte

the broadcasting might of the English Premier League enabled Man U to remain at the top of the financial league table.

Deloitte's rankings combine commercial deals such as sponsorships and shirt sales, match-day revenues and broadcast income. An ever-increasing share of clubs' turnover now comes from the latter, which reached an all-time high of 45% last year. It is no surprise, then, that English teams comprise half of the top 20. The 2016–17 season was the first of a new three-year Premier League television deal worth around £2.8bn ($4bn) per season. This is more than twice the value of the broadcasting deals struck by any of the other "big five" European leagues (those in Spain, Germany, France and Italy). As a result, Southampton FC made more money last season than AS Roma, and Leicester City's Champions League run pushed them above Inter Milan.

Overall, football is in fine financial health. Clubs' revenues rose across the board last year, with the top 20 collectively raking in €7.9bn ($9.8bn) compared with €3.9bn a decade ago. But the richest continued to pull ahead. The richest three clubs had a combined gross of €2bn, more than the total turnover of the eleven clubs ranked 20–30. And with analysts warning that the next round of football-rights auctions in Europe will be less frenzied as viewers opt for cheaper internet-video services, the market may be reaching a peak – at least for now.

Speaking my language: words and wisdom

Why emoji have beneficial linguistic side-effects

The way the world's languages are displayed digitally can be a topic of raging, if somewhat arcane, debate. Coders and designers may disagree over whether a particular script has differentiated upper and lower cases, or which set of accents it needs. But the latest discussion, about emoji (the icons used in electronic communications to convey meaning or emotion – think smiling yellow faces), has been stickier than most.

It is all to do with Unicode. This is a standard that assigns numbers and a corresponding description to the characters of the world's alphabets, as well as to many other things, such as mathematical symbols. It allows different devices, operating systems and applications to show the same characters across thousands of languages, so that a WhatsApp message written in, say, Sanskrit on an iPhone in California can be read by a recipient using a Windows laptop in Kathmandu. The standard is managed by a non-profit group, the Unicode Consortium, which began operations in the early 1990s. It regularly adds more characters to the list, whether for ancient languages that academics want to use, or for modern ones with relatively few speakers or unusual characters. The Script Encoding Initiative, which was established by the University of California, Berkeley, has a list of 100 scripts from South and South-East Asia, Africa and the Middle East that have yet to be incorporated into Unicode.

The Unicode standard started listing codes for emoji in 2010. After emerging in Japan in 1999, emoji spread worldwide in the 2000s, but no operating system or messaging app had a common numbering or representation scheme. So Windows, Android and iOS not only use different graphical renditions of those smiling yellow faces (and rice bowls, etc), but also at one time coded them with different numbers. An emoji sent from one system might appear as a completely different emoji, or even as a blank rectangular box, on arrival. Fortunately, the Unicode Consortium stepped in to standardise the numbers used, even though the specific appearance depends on the receiving platform or application (which now includes Slack, Facebook and Twitter, as well as operating systems on different devices). The difficulty for Unicode is that demand for more emoji is growing. This is driven by the likes of Apple and Google, as well as by businesses, industries, individuals and interest groups keen to see a particular symbol represented. The American state of Maine supported the proposal to add a lobster emoji. All proposals for new emoji put to the Unicode Consortium must be discussed and voted upon.

Some of the consortium's members worry that making decisions about new emoji is distracting them from more scholarly matters and delaying the addition of new characters from scripts both ancient and modern. Proposals for frowning piles of poo (the smiling version already exists) drew particular ire, and were described as "damaging ... to the Unicode standard", by Michael Everson, a typographer. Such concerns are exaggerated, however, says Mark Davis, co-founder of the Unicode Consortium. Although emoji occupy a disproportionate percentage of media attention, the consortium has created a separate committee to handle them. Mr Davis also notes that the focus on emoji has had beneficial side-effects. Many software products previously lacked Unicode support. But designers keen to incorporate emoji installed upgrades that, as a side-effect, also allowed the display of Unicode characters in hundreds of languages that would otherwise have been ignored.

How the letters of the alphabet got their names

There seems to be little predictability to the English names for the letters of the alphabet, to say nothing of the names of letters in other languages. Some begin with an e-as-in-egg sound (eff, ell); some end in an ee sound (tee, dee); and others have no obvious rhyme or reason to them at all. How did they get that way?

The vowels are all named after their long forms. In Middle English, these were roughly ah, ay (as in "may"), ee, oh, oo (as in "tool"). But the "Great Vowel Shift" scrambled the long vowels of English over several centuries, starting in around 1400. This made English vowels sound different from those in Europe, and changed the letters' names with them, to ay, ee, aye, oh. U was still called oo after the Great Vowel shift; only in around 1600 did it start being called yoo. The *Oxford English Dictionary* says of wy, also known as Y, merely that the name is of "obscure origin". It is at least 500 years old.

The names of consonants are more regular than first appears. They use a modified form of the system handed down from Latin. "Stop" consonants – those that stop the airflow entirely – get an ee sound after them (think B, D, P and T). Consonants with a continuing airflow get an e-as-in-egg sound at the beginning instead (F, L, M, N, S, X). There are a couple of exceptions. C and G have both stop and non-stop ("hard" and "soft") sounds, as seen in "cat" and "cent", and "gut" and "gin". They are called see and gee because in Latin they were only "stop" consonants and so follow the same naming rules as B and D. (Why they are not pronounced key and ghee is unclear.)

Other anomalies require a bit more explanation. R, which has a continuing airflow, used to conform to the rule above, and was called er. It changed to ar for unknown reasons. V was used as both a consonant and a vowel in Latin, and so does not fit the pattern above either: it is a fricative (a consonant in which noise is produced by disrupting the airflow), named like a stop. Double-U is a remnant of V's old double-life, too. J did not exist in Latin; its English pronunciation is inherited from French, with some alternation.

Zed comes from the Greek zeta. (Americans call it zee, perhaps to make it behave more like the other letter-names, though the exact reason is unclear.) And aitch is perhaps the greatest weirdo in the alphabet. Its name is descended from the Latin accha, ahha or aha, via the French *ache*. The modern name for the letter does not have an h-sound in it, in most places. But there is a variant – haitch – thought by some to be a "hypercorrection", an attempt to insert the letter's pronunciation into its name. In the Irish republic, haitch is considered standard; in Northern Ireland, it is used by Catholics, whereas aitch is a shibboleth that identifies Protestants. But it is not limited to Ireland: haitch is also spreading among the English young, to the horror of their elders.

Why Papua New Guinea has so many languages

India, with its 1.3bn people, vast territory and 22 official languages (along with hundreds of unofficial ones), is well known as one of the most linguistically diverse countries in the world. Yet it is no match for a country of just 7.6m inhabitants in the Pacific Ocean: Papua New Guinea. Nearly 850 languages are spoken in the country, making it the most linguistically diverse place on earth. Why does Papua New Guinea have so many languages, and how do locals cope?

The oldest group of languages in Papua New Guinea are the so-called "Papuan" languages, introduced by the first human settlers 40,000 years ago. Despite falling under the "Papuan" umbrella, these languages do not share a single root. Instead, they are split into dozens of unrelated families (and some isolates – single languages with no relatives at all). This contrasts with Papua New Guinea's Austronesian languages, which arrived some 3,500 years ago, probably from a single Taiwanese source. Things were further complicated in the 1800s by the arrival of English- and German-speaking colonists. After independence, Papua New Guinea adopted three official languages. English is the first; Tok Pisin, a creole, is the second; Hiri Motu, a simplified version of Motu, an Austronesian language, is the third. (Sign language was added in 2015.) But the lack of state recognition did not quash variety. The country's 850-odd languages each enjoy between a few dozen and 650,000 speakers.

Many of these languages have survived thanks to Papua New Guinea's wild topography. Mountains, jungles and swamps keep villagers isolated, preserving their languages. A rural population helps too: only about 13% of Papuans live in towns. Indeed, some Papuans have never had any contact with the outside world. Fierce tribal divisions – Papua New Guinea is often shaken by communal violence – also encourage people to be proud of their own languages. The passing of time is another important factor that has promoted linguistic diversity. It takes about a thousand years for a single language to split in two, says William Foley, a linguist. With 40,000 years to evolve, Papuan languages have had plenty of time to change naturally.

In the face of this incredible variety of languages, Papuans have embraced Tok Pisin, a creole based on English, but with German, Portuguese and native Papuan languages mixed in. It started as a pidgin, developed by traders in the 19th century. (Its name is a pidginisation of "talk pidgin".) But in recent decades it has become the main language in Papua New Guinea. There is a Tok Pisin newspaper, and it is popular in church. Tok Pisin is now spoken by 4m Papuans, a majority of the population. Its root as a pidgin helps explain its success: simple vocabulary makes it easy to learn. Its mixed heritage also makes it dazzlingly expressive. Pikinini means "child" and comes from Portuguese. The Tok Pisin for "urbanite" is susok man – "shoe sock man" in English. Yet Tok Pisin's success may threaten Papua New Guinea's linguistic diversity: it is also slowly crowding out other languages. A dozen have already vanished. As a modern Papuan language flourishes, ancient ones risk being lost for ever.

Is Serbo-Croatian one language or four?

Around 17m people in Bosnia, Serbia, Croatia and Montenegro speak variations of what used to be called Serbo-Croatian or Croato-Serbian. Officially, though, the language that once united Yugoslavia has, like the country, ceased to exist. Instead, it now has four names: Bosnian, Serbian, Croatian and Montenegrin. But are these really all the same language?

The answer, according to a group of linguists and NGOs from the four countries, is a resounding "yes". Working under the banner of a project called "Language and Nationalism", the group issued a "declaration on the common language" in 2017. It stated that the four tongues together form a "polycentric" language, similar to English, German or Arabic. They argue that although different dialects exist, these are variations of the same language, because everyone who speaks it can understand one another. Indeed, this makes the four tongues more similar than the dialects of many other polycentric languages. The authors consider the insistence by educational and public institutions on the usage of only one of the four name variants to be "repressive, unnecessary and harmful". The aim of the declaration is to stimulate discussion on language "without the nationalistic baggage and to contribute to the reconciliation process", said Daliborka Uljarevic, the Montenegrin partner behind the declaration.

The insistence on calling Serbo-Croatian by four different names leads to endless absurdities. Children who live in the same town in Bosnia go to school in the same building but to classes in different languages. The Bosnian government portal is published in four languages: English, Bosnian and Croatian, which are written in the Latin alphabet, and Serbian, which is written in Cyrillic script. Yet the region's politicians do not need translations when meeting. When war criminals are on trial before the UN tribunal in The Hague, they receive interpretation in the dialect spoken by the translator who happens to be on duty. A well-circulated meme from Bosnia highlights the absurdity: it features cigarette packets that repeat "smoking kills" twice in the Latin script and once in Cyrillic, all spelled identically.

As in so many parts of the world, the tussle over language is political. Nationalist Serbs see the 2017 declaration as an attempt to undermine the link between Serbs in Serbia, Bosnian Serbs and Montenegrins. Defusing the language issue would take away a tool the nationalists have used to stir trouble; it emphasises differences. Nationalist Serbs fear that if everyone thought they spoke the same language in Bosnia, that would undermine their political ambition of eventually destroying the country. Nationalist Croats trace the struggle for independence, in part, back to the struggle of academics in the 1960s who claimed that Croatian was a separate language. If it were, then Croats must be a separate people, and hence not Yugoslavs, they argued. Yet most ordinary people do not care much about the issue. When they ask if you speak their language, more often than not, they call it simply naški, "ours".

How language is bound up with national identity

The rise of populism in Europe and the United States in recent years has revealed how deeply divided voters are over immigration. Nationalists and populists, from Donald Trump to Britain's UK Independence Party and Alternative for Germany (AfD), have proclaimed that governments should make keeping foreigners out a priority. But pinning down exactly what defines a foreigner, and what defines a national, is tricky. This is partly because identity is based on a nebulous mix of values, language, history, culture and citizenship.

A poll published in February 2017 by the Pew Research Centre, a think-tank, attempted to unravel the idea of how someone can

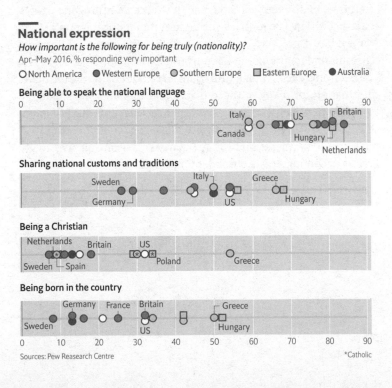

National expression

How important is the following for being truly (nationality)?
Apr–May 2016, % responding very important

○ North America ● Western Europe ◐ Southern Europe ▢ Eastern Europe ● Australia

Being able to speak the national language

0 — 10 — 20 — 30 — 40 — 50 — 60 — 70 — 80 — 90

Italy, US, Britain, Canada, Hungary, Netherlands

Sharing national customs and traditions

Sweden, Germany, Italy, US, Greece, Hungary

Being a Christian

Netherlands, Britain, US, Poland, Greece, Sweden, Spain

Being born in the country

Sweden, Germany, France, Britain, US, Greece, Hungary

0 — 10 — 20 — 30 — 40 — 50 — 60 — 70 — 80 — 90

Sources: Pew Reasearch Centre   *Catholic

be judged to be genuinely American, British or German. It asked respondents about various characteristics – language spoken, customs observed, religion and country of birth – and how important they were to being a national of their country.

On average, over the 15 countries surveyed, speaking a state's national tongue was seen as the most important trait. The Dutch rated this higher than anyone, whereas Canadians were least concerned about linguistic ability, with only half saying that being able to converse in English or French (one of the two national languages) was very important. One reason may be that Canada is divided by language; another is that, along with Australia, it had the largest share of people born abroad among the countries polled, at over 20% of the population.

Recent experiences with immigration appear to affect different countries in different ways. People in Greece and Hungary, which have been transit countries for large numbers of migrants from the Middle East, placed strikingly high importance on sharing customs and traditions, and being born in the country (Greeks also cared strongly about being Christian). Yet in Germany, the ultimate destination for many of the refugees and migrants, respondents gave comparatively little weight to such factors. That suggests that there may still be life in Germany's *Willkommenskultur* ("welcoming culture") – or at least that the AfD party still has some way to go before becoming a real contender for power.

How machines learned to process human language

Gadgets that can understand and respond to spoken commands are growing in popularity. Amazon's Echo devices, featuring a digital assistant called Alexa, can be found in millions of homes. Ask Alexa to play music, set a timer, order a taxi, tell you about your commute or tell a corny joke, and she will comply. Voice-driven digital assistants from other big tech firms (Google Assistant, Microsoft's Cortana and Apple's Siri) have also vastly improved. How did computers learn to process human language?

The original approach to getting computers to understand human language was to use sets of precise rules – for example, in translation, a set of grammar rules for breaking down the meaning of the source language, and another set for reproducing the meaning in the target language. But after a burst of optimism in the 1950s, such systems could not be made to work on complex new sentences; the rules-based approach would not scale up. Funding for so-called natural-language processing went into hibernation for decades, until a renaissance in the late 1980s.

Then a new approach emerged, based on machine learning – a technique in which computers are trained using lots of examples, rather than being explicitly programmed. For speech recognition, computers are fed sound files on the one hand, and human-written transcriptions on the other. The system learns to predict which sounds should result in what transcriptions. In translation, the training data are source-language texts and human-made translations. The system learns to match the patterns between them. One thing that improves both speech recognition and translation is a "language model" – a bank of knowledge about what (for example) English sentences tend to look like. This narrows the system's guesswork considerably. In recent years, machine-learning approaches have made rapid progress, for three reasons. First, computers are far more powerful. Second, they can learn from huge and growing stores of data, whether publicly available on the internet or privately gathered by firms. Third, so-called "deep learning" methods have combined faster computers and more abundant data with new training algorithms and more complex architectures that can learn from example even more efficiently.

All this means that computers are now impressively competent at handling spoken requests that require a narrowly defined reply. "What's the temperature going to be in London tomorrow?" is simple (though you don't need to be a computer to know it is going to rain in London tomorrow). Users can even ask in more natural ways, such as, "Should I carry an umbrella to London tomorrow?" (Digital assistants learn continually from the different ways people ask questions.) But ask a wide-open question ("Is there anything fun and inexpensive to do in London tomorrow?") and you will usually just get a list of search-engine results. As machine learning improves, and as users let their gadgets learn more about them specifically, such answers will become more useful. Privacy advocates worry about the implications of being surrounded by devices that are constantly listening. But if the past few years of smartphone use are any indication, consumers are happy to set aside such concerns in return for the convenience of being able to operate a computer simply by speaking to it. Indeed, it is rather like casting a spell: say the right words, and something happens. That is the magic of machine learning.

Why the World Bank needs to cut down on the word "and"

An unusual war of words flared up in early 2017 at the World Bank. Paul Romer, its new chief economist, was stripped of control of the research division. An internal memo claimed that the change was to bring the operations department closer to the Bank's research arm. But many suspected that it was because Mr Romer had clashed with staff over the Bank's writing style. He had demanded shorter, better-written reports. In particular, Mr Romer questioned the excessive use of the word "and". He proclaimed that he would not clear a final report for publication if "and" made up more than 2.6% of the text. His tenacious approach was said to have rubbed some employees up the wrong way. Was Mr Romer's complaint justified?

The prevalence of "and" is hardly the only or indeed the best measure of good writing style. But used to excess, it can render prose turgid or, at worst, unreadable. One of the Bank's reports from 1999 promised to "promote corporate governance and competition

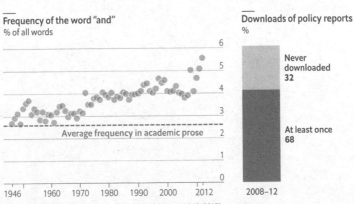

Conjunction dysfunction
World Bank reports

Frequency of the word "and"
% of all words

Average frequency in academic prose

1946 1960 1970 1980 1990 2000 2012

Downloads of policy reports
%

Never downloaded
32

At least once
68

2008–12

Sources: "Bankspeak: The Language of World Bank Reports 1946–2012" by F. Moretti and D. Pestre, 2012; World Bank

policies and reform and privatise state-owned enterprises and labour market/social protection reform." The 2.6% limit set by Mr Romer roughly matches the prevalence of "and" in academic work. (By comparison, in a typical week's print edition of *The Economist*, "and" accounts for just 1.5% of the text, excluding advertisements.)

A study by Franco Moretti and Dominique Pestre of the Stanford Literary Lab, a research outfit, analysed the language used by the World Bank since its founding in the 1940s. Back then, the average report roughly met the 2.6% standard. By 2012, however, the conjunction was taking up about 6% of the words in its reports. Other stylistic sins abounded. Acronyms had come to account for about 5% of reports, up from 3% in the 1970s. Financial terms, such as "fair value" and "portfolio", had also become more popular. The World Bank's report-writers face other difficulties, too. In 2014 the Bank's number-crunchers highlighted the unpopularity of its studies: of the 1,611 documents they assessed, 32% were never downloaded by anyone. So Mr Romer was making a good point. If the World Bank wants its reports to be read, it could at least make them a bit more readable.

The French argument over a new punctuation mark

In France, questions of language often touch off fiery national debates. In 2016 reforms meant to simplify tricky spellings – including the optional deletion of the circumflex from some words – provoked outrage and an online protest called #JeSuisCirconflexe. In 2017, another bout of linguistic anguish provoked an intervention from the prime minister and alarm from the French Academy, the official guardian of the French tongue, over a "mortal peril" to the language. It stemmed from the publication of a third-grade grammar textbook featuring a rare punctuation mark. Why did this cause such distress?

All French nouns require a gender, which is often unconnected to the thing itself. There is nothing especially masculine, for instance, about *le bureau* (the desk) or feminine about *la table* (the table). In other cases, a noun's gender is derived from the biological sex of its referent: *un directeur* is a male director; *une directrice* is a female one. Since the 17th century, the rule for plurals has been that the masculine always trumps the feminine. The reason, according to an early member of the French Academy, is that "the masculine is more noble". Therefore, if only one *directeur* joins a group of 500 *directrices*, they collectively become *les directeurs*. The grammatical dominance of the masculine in French frequently creates conflict. A commission was created in 1984 to feminise job titles in order to recognise the growing numbers of women working in traditionally male-dominated professions. Its recommendations were so detested that the French government did not make the feminisation of professions mandatory until 1998.

The disputed textbook offered a solution to what some feminists believe is an example of the sexism encoded in the French language. In order to refer to both genders, it inserts a floating dot, known as an interpunct, after the masculine version of certain plural nouns, and follows it with the feminine ending. So the group of one male and 500 female directors, for instance, becomes *les directeur·rice·s*. Few paid attention in 2015 when the High Council for Gender Equality, a consultative state body tasked with promoting equal rights, proposed the fix in a list of recommendations on implementing gender-inclusive language. The backlash to the textbook's publication was rather swifter. The (predominantly male) French Academy, created by Cardinal Richelieu in 1635, warned that this "aberration" would create "a confusion close to illegibility" and allow other languages to "take advantage to prevail". Édouard Philippe, the prime minister, weighed in, asking ministers "not to make use of the so-called inclusive writing in official texts".

The controversy over gender-inclusive language came just as France grappled with its own #MeToo protests against sexual abuse and harassment, called #BalanceTonPorc ("Expose your pig"). More than 300 French teachers signed a manifesto saying that they would no longer teach the rule that the masculine dominates the feminine. Technology, too, is playing a role in helping to regularise gender-inclusive language, despite the warning cries from the French Academy. The French Association of Normalisation, a national standard-setting body, said that it is designing a new French keyboard that will include an interpunct. There are good reasons to do so. Several studies suggest that gender-inclusive language can help reduce gender stereotyping and discrimination; others suggest a link between gendered languages and lower rates of female work-force participation. Whether or not the interpunct catches on, that is a very good point.

Seasonal selection: festivals and holidays demystified

Where new year's resolutions come from

At the start of every year millions of people make resolutions promising improvements in their lives. Alcohol is forsworn, exercise embraced, hobbies sought. But though it may make sense to respond to the indulgences of Christmas with catharsis, the tradition of new-year resolutions is far older than the establishment of the Christian festival, or even the placing of the new year in the middle of winter.

The Babylonians were the first civilisation to leave records of new-year festivities, some 4,000 years ago. Their years were linked to agricultural seasons, with each new year beginning around the spring equinox (late March, by our modern calendar). A 12-day festival to celebrate the renewal of life, known as Akitu, marked the beginning of the agrarian year. During Akitu people keen to curry favour with the gods would promise to repay their debts and to return borrowed objects. In a similar vein the ancient Egyptians would make sacrifices to Hapi, the god of the Nile, at the beginning of their year in July, a time when the Nile's annual flood would usher in a particularly fertile period. Offering sacrifices and prayers, they would request good fortune, rich harvests or military successes.

The Romans continued the habit, but also changed the date. The Roman year is said to have originally had ten months, starting in March around the spring equinox, plus another 60-odd winter days that were not included in the named months. Around 700BC, two more months were added, but it was not until 46BC, when Julius Caesar introduced a reformed calendar, that January was officially established as the beginning of the year. Because this was the date on which the city's newly elected consuls began their tenure, it marked a shift in calendric emphasis from agrarian cycles to civil rotations. Roman new-year festivities included the worship of Janus, the god of beginnings and endings, after whom the month of January is named. But the persistence of these traditions annoyed later Christians, and in medieval Europe attempts were made to celebrate the new year on dates of religious significance, such as

Christmas, or the Feast of the Annunciation in March. Attitudes to resolutions also changed. Prayer vigils and confessions were used to pledge allegiance to religious values. At the end of Christmas feasts, some knights were said to have taken an oath known as "The Vow of the Peacock", in which they placed their hands on a peacock (a bird considered noble) in order to renew their commitment to chivalry. This moral flavour to the pledges persisted. A 17th-century Scotswoman wrote in her diary of taking Biblical verses as starting points for resolutions ("I will not offend anymore").

By the time the phrase "new-year resolutions" first appeared, in a Boston newspaper in 1813, the pledges were losing their religious overtones. An article published a few years earlier in *Walker's Hibernian Magazine, Or, Compendium of Entertaining Knowledge*, an Irish publication, satirises the practice. It states that doctors had solemnly pledged to "be very moderate in their fees" and statesmen to "have no other object in view than the good of their country". Yet the making of unrealistic, over-optimistic pledges has remained a tradition. According to polls, around half the population of Britain and America now make resolutions – but, with less fear of divine retribution to motivate them, fewer than 10% keep them.

How St Patrick's Day celebrations went global

Every March, for about a week, Dublin's corridors of power empty out. Government ministers and officials pack their bags as part of an annual soft-power push like no other. They head abroad on promotional trips linked to St Patrick's Day, the Irish national holiday that falls on March 17th. Dozens of countries play host to high-ranking Irish officials, and many more will stage their own celebrations of Irishness. The highlight of this diplomatic assault is the annual meeting between the Irish taoiseach, as the prime minister is known, and the president of the United States. Few countries enjoy such high-level access and exposure on their national day. But how did the celebration of a devout fifth-century missionary become a global phenomenon – one in which people drink Irish whiskey, dress up in green and demand that people kiss them because they are Irish (even if they are not)?

St Patrick's Day is an international celebration because of emigration. During and after the famines that afflicted Ireland in the 19th century, some 2m people left the island, the majority settling in America and Britain. By the 1850s, the Irish accounted for up to a quarter of the population of cities like Liverpool and Boston. Within these communities, an Irish identity emerged, based on a strong Catholic faith and the political cause of the day: independence from Britain. This nationalist identity was especially celebrated on St Patrick's Day when, in America and elsewhere, public sermons and speeches celebrating Irish heritage became common. In 1852, the Catholic archbishop of New York noted that not only do the Irish "cherish fond memory for the apostle of their native land, but they propagate it, and make the infection as if it were contagious".

Soon the contagion caught on. By the mid-20th century the holiday had evolved into a celebration of all things Irish, and was well established across America. With some 40m Americans claiming Irish heritage it also presented an opportunity for American politicians to curry favour among the diaspora. Irish migrants had long been victims of prejudice, but that changed as the

20th century wore on. The wariness shown in job advertisements declaring "Irish need not apply" gave way to a more positive image of witty types, who were not averse to an occasional glass of the strong stuff. This helped to fuel the idea of St Patrick's Day as an excuse for a party. That the Irish had managed to work their way up the social ladder in the cities where they made their home added to their image as plucky underdogs.

In Dublin, the national festival can bring in as much as €70m ($87m), according to one estimate. And now there is the Global Greening, in which landmarks from the Great Wall of China to the Eiffel Tower in Paris are bathed in green light. Celebrations have even been held on the International Space Station. Business deals are struck on trade missions and dignitaries take the opportunity to be snapped having the craic with pints of Guinness in their hands. Pubs heave, parades march and for one day revellers raise a glass to Ireland and its globalising patron saint.

Why Easter moves around so much

Unlike other Christian holidays, Easter can move around a lot from one year to the next, its date sometimes varying by more than a month. It falls between March 22nd and April 25th for the Western church, and between April 4th and May 8th for the Eastern church. This in turn determines the dates of public holidays, school holidays and the timings of school terms in many countries. Why does Easter move around so much? Be warned: the answer is rather technical.

According to the Bible, Jesus held the Last Supper with his disciples on the night of the Jewish festival of Passover, died the next day (Good Friday) and rose again on the third day (ie, two days later, on the Sunday). The beginning of Passover is determined by the first full moon after the vernal equinox, which can occur on any day of the week. To ensure that Easter occurs on a Sunday, the Council of Nicaea therefore ruled in 325AD that Easter would be celebrated on the Sunday after the first full moon on or after the vernal equinox. But there's a twist: if the full moon falls on a Sunday, then Passover begins on a Sunday, so Easter is then delayed by a week to ensure that it still occurs after Passover. To confuse matters further, the council fixed the date of the vernal equinox at March 21st, the date on which it occurred in 325AD (it occurs on or around March 20th), and introduced a set of tables to define when the full moon occurs that do not quite align with the actual astronomical full moon (which means that, in practice, Easter can actually occur before Passover).

The earliest possible date for Easter occurs when the notional full moon falls on March 21st itself, in a year in which March 21st falls on a Saturday. Easter is then celebrated on Sunday March 22nd, a rare event that last happened in 1818 and will next take place in 2285. The latest possible date for Easter occurs when there is a full moon on March 20th, so that the first full moon after March 21st falls a lunar month or 29 days later, on April 18th. If April 18th falls on a Sunday, then the special Sunday rule applies, and Easter is celebrated the following Sunday, or April 25th. This last happened in 1943, and will next happen in 2038. There is therefore a 35-day window in which Easter can fall, depending on the timing of the full moon relative to March 21st. Eastern Christianity applies the same basic rule but uses the older Julian calendar, which is currently 13 days behind the Gregorian calendar, giving a different range of possible dates. This can pose problems.

There have been various proposals to change the way the date of Easter is calculated. At a meeting held in Aleppo in 1997, representatives of several churches proposed that a new system be adopted from 2001, relying on actual astronomical observations rather than tables to define the dates of the vernal equinox and the full moon. This would have ensured that Easter occurred on the same day for both branches of the church. But the proposal was not adopted. In 1928 Britain's parliament passed a law, which has not been implemented, that would define Easter as the Sunday after the second Saturday in April. Another proposal would define Easter as the second Sunday in April. Several churches, including the Catholic church, say they are open to the idea of setting the date of Easter in this way, so that its date varies by no more than a week. But until there is widespread agreement, its date will continue to jump around within a five-week window.

Why Europeans slack off in August

Do you need to see a dentist, get some building work done, or buy a loaf of bread? If you live in continental Europe, you will know that trying to do any of these things in August is generally not a good idea. A surprising number of businesses observe the long-established tradition of closing their doors for the whole month (though some prefer to do so in July). Pictures of hammocks and palm trees adorn the websites of small businesses across the continent, wishing customers a happy holiday and advising them to come back again in September. "Summer is near and Frankie will take a nap for a while," says the site of Frankie's Social, a bar in Limassol, Cyprus, without giving any indication of when it might open again. Why do Europeans take off August en masse?

The idea that summer is for play, not work, seems hard to shake for many Europeans. The habit is especially ingrained in old manufacturing sectors. During and after the industrial revolution, entire factories in northern England would decamp to the same beachside resorts. Until the 1980s Volkswagen, a German carmaker, would charter trains at the start of summer break to move thousands of Italian workers from its plants in Wolfsburg, which turned into a ghost town, to their homes in Italy. One reason is that an assembly line does not function very well without a full complement of workers, so it makes sense for them all to take time off together. It is also a good opportunity to perform any maintenance or upgrades on the factory floor.

Yet the practice of downing tools in the midst of summer has spread well beyond the industrial sphere. It is harder to apply the same logic to restaurants and cafés, particularly those serving tourists. "We are open the rest of the year, seven days a week, so these days are earned," says Rita Zubelli, who works in an ice-cream parlour in Milan that, bafflingly, shuts down at the height of the summer. In such sectors the practice of a shut-down seems driven more by habit, and the social acceptance of holidaymaking at that time, than by business logic.

If you are a tourist looking for an ice-cream, a local trying to find a plumber, or even a journalist trying to write a story, Europe's attitude to summer can be deeply frustrating. Yet despite, or perhaps because of, their leisure-seeking ways, Europeans are the most productive workers in the world. Dan Rogers of Peakon, a consultancy, thinks the dip in employee productivity over holiday periods could be a good reason to accept the European summer. From an employer's perspective, he says, "if your employees are less productive, and your business partners less responsive, the sensible decision would be to shut up shop".

How Thanksgiving became a secular holiday

Every November, tens of millions of Americans crisscross their country to spend Thanksgiving with family and friends. With any luck, turkey, pumpkin pie and good cheer await. The story of the celebration is enshrined in American lore. In November 1620 a group of English Pilgrims landed at Cape Cod, Massachusetts, after two months aboard the *Mayflower*. They were helped through the deprivations of their first winter by local Wampanoag Indians, who offered provisions and advice. After a successful harvest the next year, 50 Pilgrims and 90 Indians celebrated with a turkey feast. The rest is supposedly history. But history is full of half-truths, and Thanksgiving is no exception. The way Americans celebrate the holiday today – as an annual, secular event – is a 19th-century invention.

The Pilgrims were a stern bunch. Holidays were scarce. Celebrating Christmas, Easter or saints' days was forbidden. Instead, Pilgrims observed days of public fast or thanksgiving. These were proclaimed in response to specific events, and therefore varied each year. It was believed that fasting could temper a looming crisis, such as a drought or invasion, while thanksgiving marked a good harvest or military victory. Prayer was at the heart of these events. Evidence about the gathering in 1621, albeit just four sentences long, comes from a letter by the Pilgrims' leader, Edward Winslow. Wampanoag Indians appeared along with their chief, Massasoit, "whom for three days we entertained and feasted". Pilgrims made no mention of the event in later years (which was not a thanksgiving in the proper sense, since it involved no prayer) and relations with the Indians quickly soured. Within a generation they were at war. The Pilgrims won, and in 1676 declared a day of thanks, displaying the impaled head of Massasoit's son – "meat to the people inhabiting the wilderness", in the words of one Pilgrim. New Englanders continued to observe days of thanksgiving over the next 200 years, carrying the custom with them as they moved to the south and the west.

The holiday gradually assumed a semi-fixed status. Mostly it was celebrated as a local or statewide affair initiated by a minister or governor. It might be held in October, November, December or even January. A few national holidays were proclaimed in America: George Washington created one to mark the adoption of the Constitution in 1789; James Madison did so to celebrate the end of the War of 1812. But the credit for securing a fixed day for Thanksgiving, annually and nationwide, goes to an unflagging writer called Sarah Josepha Hale. She rarely alluded to the Pilgrims herself as she pursued the idea of a patriotic celebration for autumn over the course of two decades. She petitioned presidents and governors, and *Godey's Lady's Book*, her popular women's periodical, ran editorials and moralising fiction championing the cause. Success came in 1863 during the civil war. The president, Abraham Lincoln, declared the day a national holiday after victories for the Unionist armies at Gettysburg and Vicksburg earlier that year. In 1941 Congress wrote the holiday into law, to be celebrated on the fourth Thursday in November.

Nationwide observance of Thanksgiving meant that the holiday became an increasingly secular affair. In 1878 the *New York Times* complained that the day had "lost its sombreness and with that most of its religious significance". Local parades were held, with Macy's staging its first in 1924. For Hale, the holiday was the "best exponent ... of the prosperity and happiness of the American people". It was a day to celebrate abundance and instil American values: patriotism, devotion to family and hard work. Never mind that the Pilgrims would have barely recognised (and would probably have disavowed) the modern celebration. What was needed was a founding myth for a young nation.

How weather, religion and daylight hours affect Christmas music consumption

Christmas pop songs are a genre in their own right, and a money-spinner at that. By the end of 2017 the 13 most popular Christmas songs on Spotify, a music-streaming service, had amassed 1bn plays between them. The most popular of them, *All I Want for Christmas Is You*, written in 15 minutes and recorded by Mariah Carey in 1994, accounted for 210m of those plays, having earned over $60m in royalties since its release.

Despite its ubiquity during December, the appeal of festive music varies significantly by geography. Analysis of data from Spotify, covering pre-Christmas listening in 2016 across 35 countries, and for every American state, reveals that music lovers in Sweden and Norway listen to festive tunes most frequently. One in every six songs they streamed on Spotify during December 2016 received this classification (the list includes some 1,500 Christmas songs performed in English and local languages). By contrast, during the same period in Brazil – a country with a comparable proportion of Christians – just one song in 150 was Christmas-themed. Listening habits in American states also varied, though to a smaller degree: in New Hampshire Christmas songs accounted for one in nine streams, whereas in Nevada, the state where such tunes are least common, it was one in 20.

What might cause these differences between Spotify users' appetites for festive-themed music? Daylight hours, weather and religiosity appear to be big drivers of behaviour. After accounting for the amount of time remaining before Christmas and the day of the week – festive songs are most popular at the weekend – it turns out that Christmas listening is most prevalent in countries that have the fewest daylight hours and the wettest weather. For countries in the northern hemisphere, every additional hour of darkness is correlated with a three-percentage-point increase in the amount of Christmas listening on Spotify. The weather affects festive spirits too. Rainy days increase Christmas listening by 0.5 percentage

Do they know it's Christmas?

Streaming of Christmas songs per day*, as % of total music streaming, 2016

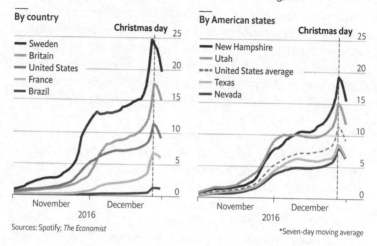

By country

Christmas day

— Sweden
— Britain
— United States
— France
— Brazil

By American states

Christmas day

— New Hampshire
— Utah
--- United States average
— Texas
— Nevada

November   December
2016

November   December
2016

Sources: Spotify; *The Economist*

*Seven-day moving average

points over dry days. In America, festive listening appears similarly fickle across states. An additional hour of darkness increases listening by 1.5 percentage points, and colder weather brings a slight increase in listening. The biggest bump is reserved for snowfall, which causes a two-percentage-point increase in streaming. And states that are more pious – measured by the percentage of people in the state that report attending weekly worship – have a greater propensity to listen to Christmas-themed music.

That the weather and daylight hours drive consumer behaviour is not surprising. Walmart, America's biggest retailer, has long known that sales of strawberry-flavoured Pop-Tarts, a snack food, rise sevenfold ahead of a hurricane. But daylight, weather and religiosity together explain only about 50% of the variation of Christmas music between countries and between states; what explains the rest of it is unclear. But the implications for the music industry are clear: snow and rain boost consumption, and thus royalties. A mild winter in November and December, with 20%

fewer snow days than average, would reduce royalties from Ms Carey's infectious hit by about $10,000. She, and other composers of festive songs, are no doubt dreaming of a white Christmas.

How Christmas, once a raucous carnival, was domesticated

There were no neatly wrapped presents. Nor were there tinselled trees or Santa Claus. Christmas in pre-industrial Europe and America looked very different from today's iteration. Drunks, cross-dressers and rowdy carollers roamed the streets. The tavern, rather than the home or the church, was the place to celebrate. "Men dishonour Christ more in the twelve days of Christmas, than in all the twelve months besides" despaired Hugh Latimer, chaplain to King Edward VI, in the mid-1500s. Some 200 years later, across the Atlantic, a Puritan minister decried the "lewd gaming" and "rude revelling" of Christmastime in the colonies. Those concerns seem irrelevant now. By the end of the 19th century, a rambunctious, freewheeling holiday had turned into the peaceable, family-centred one we know today. How did this change come about?

In early modern Europe, between about 1500 and 1800, the Christmas season meant a lull in agricultural work and a chance to indulge. The harvest had been gathered and the animals slaughtered (the cold weather meant they would not spoil). The celebration involved heavy eating, drinking and wassailing, in which peasants would arrive at the houses of the neighbouring gentry and demand to be fed. One drinking song captured the mood: "And if you don't open up your door / We will lay you flat upon the floor." Mostly this was tolerated in good humour – a kind of ritualised disorder, when the social hierarchy was temporarily inverted. Not everyone was so tolerant. In colonial Massachusetts, between 1659 and 1681, Puritans banned Christmas. They expunged the day from their almanacs, and offending revellers risked a five-shilling fine. But the ban did not last, so efforts to tame the holiday picked up instead. Moderation was advised. One almanac-writer cautioned in 1761 that "The temperate man enjoys the most delight / For riot dulls and palls the appetite". Still, Christmas was a public ritual, enacted in the tavern or street and often fuelled by alcohol.

That soon changed. Cities expanded at the start of the 19th

century to absorb the growing number of factory workers. Vagrancy and urban poverty became more common. Rowdiness at Christmas could turn violent, with bands of drunken men roaming the streets. It's little surprise that members of the upper classes saw a threat in the festivity. In his study of the holiday, Stephen Nissenbaum, a historian, credits a group of patrician writers and editorialists in America with recasting it as a domestic event. They refashioned European traditions, like Christmas trees from Germany, or Christmas boxes from England in which the wealthy would present cash or leftovers to their servants. St Nicholas, or Santa Claus, whose December name day coincided with the Christmas season, became the holiday's mascot. Clement Clarke Moore's poem *A Visit from St Nicholas,* first published in 1823, helped popularise his image. In it, a jolly Santa descends via reindeer-pulled sleigh to surprise children with presents on Christmas Eve. Newspapers also played their part. "Let all avoid taverns and grog shops for a few days," advised the *New York Herald* in 1839. Better to focus, it suggested, on "the domestic hearth, the virtuous wife, the innocent, smiling, merry-hearted children".

It was a triumph of middle-class values, and a coup for shop-owners. "Christmas is the merchant's harvest time," a retail magazine enthused in 1908. "It is up to him to garner in as big a crop of dollars as he can." Soon this new approach to Christmas would become a target of criticism in its own right, as commercialised and superficial. Nevertheless, it lives on. Merry Christmas.

Contributors

The editor wishes to thank the authors and data journalists who created the explainers and accompanying graphics on which this book is based:

Ryan Avent, Memphis Barker, Ananyo Bhattacharya, Jennifer Brown, Will Brown, Joel Budd, Geoffrey Carr, Slavea Chankova, Amanda Coletta, Tim Cross, Josie Delap, Graham Douglas, Doug Dowson, Matthieu Favas, Glenn Fleishman, James Fransham, Tom Gardner, Hallie Golden, Lane Greene, Melissa Heikkila, Hal Hodson, Charlotte Howard, Miranda Johnson, Tim Judah, Abhishek Kumar, Soumaya Keynes, Jack Lahart, Ana Lankes, Sarah Leo, Rachel Lloyd, David McKelvey, Matt McLean, Adam Meara, Sacha Nauta, John O'Sullivan, John Parker, Lloyd Parker, Ted Plafker, Stanley Pignal, Simon Rabinovitch, Adam Roberts, Jonathan Rosenthal, Rachel Savage, Guy Scriven, Alex Selby-Boothroyd, Jane Shaw, Rachana Shanbogue, Ludwig Siegele, Adam Smith, James Tozer, Henry Tricks, Andrea Valentino, Vendeline von Bredow, Tom Wainwright, Kennett Werner, Eleanor Whitehead, Callum Williams, Sam Winter Levy, Simon Wright, Pip Wroe and Wade Zhou.

For more explainers and charts from *The Economist*, visit economist. com

Index

B B S

PublicAffairs is a publishing house founded in 1997. It is a tribute to the standards, values, and flair of three persons who have served as mentors to countless reporters, writers, editors, and book people of all kinds, including me.

I. F. STONE, proprietor of *I. F. Stone's Weekly*, combined a commitment to the First Amendment with entrepreneurial zeal and reporting skill and became one of the great independent journalists in American history. At the age of eighty, Izzy published *The Trial of Socrates*, which was a national bestseller. He wrote the book after he taught himself ancient Greek.

BENJAMIN C. BRADLEE was for nearly thirty years the charismatic editorial leader of *The Washington Post*. It was Ben who gave the *Post* the range and courage to pursue such historic issues as Watergate. He supported his reporters with a tenacity that made them fearless and it is no accident that so many became authors of influential, best-selling books.

ROBERT L. BERNSTEIN, the chief executive of Random House for more than a quarter century, guided one of the nation's premier publishing houses. Bob was personally responsible for many books of political dissent and argument that challenged tyranny around the globe. He is also the founder and longtime chair of Human Rights Watch, one of the most respected human rights organizations in the world.

•   •   •

For fifty years, the banner of Public Affairs Press was carried by its owner Morris B. Schnapper, who published Gandhi, Nasser, Toynbee, Truman, and about 1,500 other authors. In 1983, Schnapper was described by *The Washington Post* as "a redoubtable gadfly." His legacy will endure in the books to come.

Peter Osnos, *Founder*

EAGLE VALLEY LIBRARY DISTRICT
P.O. BOX 240   600 BROADWAY
EAGLE, CO 81631   (970) 328-8800